about the authors

Few persons could be better qualified to write about learning the grand game of golf than *Virginia L. Nance* (Mrs. Edward K.). She has participated in all levels of competition, from a youngster in local and junior events to the major amateur women's tournaments, including the U.S. Amateur for Women. She has been medalist, semifinalist, runner-up, and winner of many tournaments.

But Mrs. Nance has excelled even more as a teacher, giving both private and class lessons to boys and girls, men and women, in high schools, at golf-practice ranges, in camps, and at colleges and universities. She has conducted numerous clinics for students and teachers at local, state, and national levels. Mrs. Nance is a Class A Teaching and Life Member of the Ladies Professional Golf Association. She has been a contributor of articles for DGWS and AAHPER publications. She holds degrees from the University of Illinois and the University of Wisconsin and has completed further graduate work at the University of Southern California.

Dr. Elwood Craig Davis, co-author, is a well-known and distinguished professor of physical education, having been associated with major institutions such as Pennsylvania State University, University of Pittsburgh, University of Louisville, and professor emeritus at University of Southern California. His last teaching was at California State University at Northridge. His honors are legion, the most outstanding perhaps being a recipient of the Phi Epsilon Kappa National Award and both the American Academy of Physical Education's Hetherington Award and the AAHPER's Luther Halsey Gulick Medal.

Dr. Davis is a graduate of the University of Washington, University of Chicago, and Columbia University. Service was in U.S. Naval Aviation and Naval Physical Training. He is the author or co-author of nine books and numerous articles.

EXPLORING SPORTS SERIES

GOLF

Revised Edition

Virginia Lindblad Nance
Elwood Craig Davis

wcb
Wm. C. Brown Company Publishers
Dubuque, Iowa

Consulting Editor

Aileene Lockhart
Texas Woman's University

Physical Education Activities
Evaluation Materials Editor

Jane A. Mott
Texas Woman's University

Interior illustrations: Ruth Schonhorst and Denise Powell

Cover photo: David Lissy/Atoz Images

Library of Congress Catalog Card Number: 82-82956

ISBN: 0-697-00986-6

Printed in the United States of America
10 9 8 7 6 5 4 3 2 1

contents

preface

This, the fifth edition of GOLF, continues its dual objectives: to present the golf strokes in a simple but thorough way so that the reader may become a more enlightened student of the game—better able to learn and develop skill in the strokes; and, to present information that will enable the reader to become well-grounded in the knowledges of the game of golf.

The current edition has been considerably revised; however, we have retained the general outline for presenting the golf strokes as well as the knowledges of the game. All of the writing and the illustrations in the previous edition have been carefully examined. Some of the writing has been expanded, some shortened—all for the purpose of achieving clarity. Some new illustrations have been added; others of previous editions revised.

The important chapter on safety has been enlarged and now includes precautions on operating a motorized cart. We feel that this text performs a unique service by including this section. We have seen new students become teachers overnight: golf has a way of stirring up enthusiasm—enthusiasm to teach a relative or friend. It is essential that these "new teachers" (and their students) know and observe safety precautions. Also, on some golf courses we continue to see careless practices that endanger players. We hope, through this chapter on safety, that we can help achieve the goal of making golf an even safer game.

The rules of etiquette have been revised and expanded. With this thorough detailed account and with our final words, "An Afterword, You and the Game of Golf," we continue the crusade to influence players to practice good golf etiquette—to show respect, thus making it possible for all golfers to enjoy their games.

The summary of rules has been brought up to date with the new rule changes. The true-false and completion test at the end of the book has been revised. We have intentionally avoided making the test a simple one; we believe that readers of this book want to acquire a thorough knowledge of accepted practices and rules. The test should lead readers to study the USGA Rule Book and thereby gain a complete and thorough understanding of the rules.

The chapter on "Improving Your Golf Game" has been enlarged. Ranging from "Attitude and Concentration" through "Instructions for the New Player," it is a potpourri of thoughts and suggestions. For golfers who carefully study their games and enjoy keeping records of scores, a system of charting 18-hole and Target Scores for each hole is presented. This charting, besides being interesting, should help players avoid two problems: "playing" an opponent and "getting down" when they score poorly on one or two holes. "Some Thoughts on Fitness in Golf" provides ideas on getting the most out of golf and using the body effectively, rather than abusing it. Common stroke errors are studied, and the reader is urged to join in thinking through the causes and examining possible corrective measures for poor golf shots. Players should not be thoroughly mystified by shot errors; we believe they can do a lot to help themselves. Yet, we also recognize the importance of having a competent instructor observe the swing and make corrections. We, the authors, cannot see the error: we readily admit our limitations.

Our original concept of presenting the golf strokes has been retained. After establishing a sound base of understanding certain fundamentals of learning and some mechanics of swinging the club, the text then progresses to learning the grip, the stance, and the swings—working from the simple to the complex. In presenting the strokes, emphasis continues to be on moving the club with a purpose, rather than on numerous details of body action.

We continue to try to steer players toward correct paths as they attempt to gain skill. We warn against too much emphasis on detail and the "hows" of swinging a club. We urge players to follow the practices of the experts, such as working on tempo and rhythm, and on developing one swing that can be trusted to repeat, and repeat. We warn against experimentation and "tension." The cues and suggestions for swinging a club, together with the many practice ideas, can help players improve their games.

As any book of this type must be, this one is intended to be a supplement to golf instruction. Because so many theories exist about the golf swing, no single book is all-inclusive. The reader should not conclude that concepts and ideas omitted from this writing are necessarily questioned or rejected.

To try to do justice to the history of the game in a few paragraphs is impossible. Therefore, we urge the reader to go to other sources to study the interesting history of golf. Reference books and encyclopedias offer good factual accounts. But to savor, enjoy, and appreciate the history of the game, nothing can surpass reading the works of golfers and writers who lived in, and described golf's historic years. The colorful language; the illustrations; the descriptions of courses, players, equipment, technique, and play—all add up to enjoyable and profitable reading.

We express our appreciation to the teachers and golfers who have given us their comments and criticisms. We have carefully studied their suggestions and incorporated some of them.

We hope the presentations made in this book on the skills and knowledges of the game will contribute to making golf your lifetime recreation.

the game of golf

1

Golf is a game, a profession, a business asset, a social activity, and often a humiliating experience. The "put-down" that golf imposes on all players may be its fascination. Golf teases you. It can lift you into ecstatic worlds where you dream of playing perfect golf. Then without warning your dreams are shattered—golf has put you in your place. Time and again the game seems to delight in proving that you can only be its devotee—not its master. After your visions of playing great golf are dimmed, you manage to stroke some shots with unusual skill. Again you are coaxed back into the imaginary world of perfect golf. Such is the lure of golf—sampling the joy of hitting fine shots and enjoying great hopes, followed by disappointments, and then renewed hopes. The spirit and desire to attempt to conquer this challenging game survive despite all of its vicissitudes.

You either are one of the millions of people playing golf or you soon will be. It is not necessary to "sell" golf. The advantages of knowing how to play are evident. Ever-increasing numbers of people choose to learn the game and once chosen, golf becomes an enjoyable, lifetime recreation.

THE GAME

The object of golf is to play a round, usually 18 holes, in as few strokes as possible. At the beginning of each hole, the *tee* or *teeing area,* it is permissible to place the ball on a peg *(tee)* so it is slightly elevated from the turf. After the ball is struck from the tee, *it is a cardinal rule of golf that the ball be played as it lies on the ground* (except as otherwise provided by the rules). Generally four golfers, commonly called a *foursome,* play in a group. These players, after teeing off, continue playing their shots in turn (farthest from the hole playing first) until they stroke each of their golf balls into the *hole (cup).* The hole is sunk in a carpet-like area, the *putting green.* A *flagstick* is placed in the center of the cup so that the position of the hole can be seen from a distance. Some courses will have the hole number printed on the pennant of the stick.

The area of mowed grass between the tee and the putting green is called the *fairway.* The game would be relatively simple if the ball only had to be played from the tee, the fairway, and the putting green. But such is not the case. If a

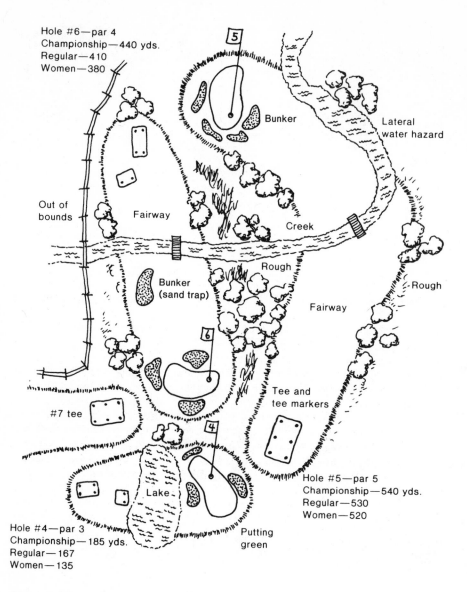

Hole #6—par 4
Championship—440 yds.
Regular—410
Women—380

Bunker

Lateral
water hazard

Out of
bounds

Fairway

Creek

Rough

Bunker
(sand trap)

Rough

Fairway

Tee and
tee markers

#7 tee

Hole #5—par 5
Championship—540 yds.
Regular—530
Women—520

Lake

Putting
green

Hole #4—par 3
Championship—185 yds.
Regular—167
Women—135

Fig. 1.1. Three golf holes

shot is hit off line and off the fairway, the ball is likely to be found among trees and in long, thick grass—the *rough*. Also, *hazards* such as *lakes, creeks,* and *bunkers* (sand traps) lie ready to engulf misjudged and errant shots.

After play on each hole is completed, the number of strokes a player has taken is recorded on the score card. (see Etiquette, Putting Green). Scores are added for the first and second nine holes *(front* and *back nines)* and then totaled for the 18-hole score.

Play U.S.G.A. Rules except as modified by Local Rules.   Please Observe Rules of Etiquette.

	1	2	3	4	5	6	7	8	9	OUT	10	11	12	13	14	15	16	17	18	IN	TOTAL	HDCP	NET
Yards - Championship - Blue	525	430	405	185	540	440	160	380	440	3505	505	420	180	535	455	210	400	435	442	3582	7087		
Regular White	510	415	400	167	530	410	150	370	420	3372	490	385	165	520	423	185	375	415	428	3386	6758		
PAR	5	4	4	3	5	4	3	4	4	36	5	4	3	5	4	3	4	4	4	36	72		
Handicap*	11	5	15	7	9	1	13	17	3		10	16	14	8	2	12	18	6	4				
HOLE	1	2	3	4	5	6	7	8	9	OUT	10	11	12	13	14	15	16	17	18	IN	TOTAL	HDCP	NET
Yards - Women Red	480	375	395	135	520	380	147	365	380	3177	470	360	140	510	375	180	370	395	415	3215	6392		
PAR	5	4	4	3	5	4	3	4	4	36	5	4	3	5	4	3	4	4	5	37	73		
Handicap*	5	13	1	17	3	11	7	15	9		8	12	18	6	16	4	14	2	10				

Date _____   Scorer_____   Attest _____

Course Rating**
Men 69.8 - Women 70.6

Please Replace Divots....Repair Ball Marks on Greens....Rake Sand Traps
Slow Players Must Allow Following Group To Play Through

*Handicap—These numbers indicate the ranking of the golf holes in order of difficulty. Hole #6, HDCP. rating #1, is considered the most difficult hole for men. Hole #3 is rated the most difficult for women. Holes #16 and #12, HDCP. rating #18 for men and women respectively, are considered the least difficult.

**Course Rating—Evaluation of the playing difficulty of a course compared with other rated courses.

Fig. 1.2. Score card

Par—The Ever-Present Opponent

Par scores are good scores. The score card shows the par for each hole, the total for both nines, and the 18-hole total. Experienced golfers aim to shoot par or less on each hole.

Interesting terms are used to describe scores in relation to par for a hole. Check score card (fig. 1.2) for these scores: On Hole 13, a score of 4, one under par, is a *birdie;* on Hole 16, a score of 2, two under par, is an *eagle;* on Hole 7, a score of 4, one over par, is a *bogey.* A *double bogey* is two over par for a hole. An exceptionally good score, rarer than a hole-in-one, is a *double eagle,* three under par.

The major guide in determining par for a hole is the distance of the hole. The number of strokes a good player needs to hit the ball onto the putting green is figured and then two strokes are added for play on the green. On the average, men hit the ball farther than women do, so women's par will differ from men's par on some of the holes.

COMPUTATION OF PAR

	Women		Men
Par		Par	
3	up to 210 yards	3	up to 250 yards
4	211–400	4	251–470
5	401–575	5	471 and over
6	576 and over		

A Challenge Requiring Self-Discipline and Concentration

Golf is a personal game. From the time the ball is hit from the first tee until it is removed from the hole on the eighteenth green, players are in command of their own games. There is no reaction to someone else's play, such as in tennis and handball. In golf, if the ball is missed completely or is poorly hit, the incident cannot be dismissed, as in some sports, by saying the opponent hit a superb shot. No excuses are allowed. But when golfers hit excellent shots they are rewarded— they can claim credit for fine play.

Golf is played in a quiet atmosphere where players may be sensitive to everything both inside and outside themselves. Having time to think in silent surroundings adds a singular dimension—one demanding concentration and self-discipline. A shot is seldom played without some thought. This is not the case in many games where brilliant plays may be or must be executed as a result of rapid-fire reaction only. Golfers must plan their play, control their thinking, initiate and complete the action in order to play each shot. They have time to be introspective—which can be either a detriment or an advantage. They can even "talk" themselves into a bad shot, or a good shot.

Directing the thinking process is a necessity and a real exercise in self-control. Anxious or negative thoughts, fearful of the shot result, must be avoided or blocked out; positive thoughts with trust for a good shot must be embraced. Before the stroke is taken, the thinking mind does its work of planning the shot and instilling confidence—then this mind must be quieted and relinquish its control to the subconscious for automatic performance. The execution of the shot should proceed at once, with no thought interjected and no plan changed. This is not a simple task.

The physical and mental aspects of golf are interwoven. Together they make a golf game. The challenge to hit good shots is always present and when accomplished—always a joy.

GOLF COURSES

Much expert knowledge and work go into planning, building, and maintaining a golf course. Sometimes the playing of the game is so absorbing or exasperating that the beauty and design of a golf course are momentarily forgotten. Golf requires the largest playing field of any modern game. All courses and all holes differ. Golf course architects design courses to challenge players to hit their best shots and to penalize them if they fail to do so. The designers lay out the courses, taking full advantage of the topography, the beauty of nature and the outdoors.

On what may be called standard for a golf course, holes vary in length from about 100 yards to about 600 yards. Since golf does not have an exact regulation playing field, golfers must continually adapt their games to the peculiarities of each course, which may in itself vary in length and challenge from day to day. To protect the turf on the teeing area and around the cup on the putting green, the *tee markers* and the cups are shifted often. If the teeing areas and putting greens are large, the placement of both tee markers and cups can make a significant difference in the difficulty and the lengths of the holes.

Some golf courses have unusually long teeing areas or have more than one tee per hole. On these courses three sets of *tee markers* may be set up: blue markers for the back tees—the championship course; white markers for the middle tees—the regular course; and, red markers for the front tees—the women's course. (The colors of the markers may vary from course to course.) Many courses have only two sets of tees, regular and women's tees.

The changing of the cups on the putting greens from flat to various undulating surfaces adds challenge and zest to the game. On many courses, especially those bordering the ocean or in the mountains, the ball may roll over the slanting surfaces in a direction exactly opposite to the one decided on by the player. The story is told that after one man played an ocean side course for the first time, he became so frustrated trying to figure out the roll of the ball on the greens that he returned the next day with a carpenter's level to check the slopes of the putting greens. (The rules of golf do not permit the use of such a device.)

Courses having all relatively short holes (executive and par-3 courses) offer certain advantages to the novice. A simpler version of golf is played, thus more success and pleasure are possible for the beginners. For all players these short courses are challenging, offer practice in the important short game, and require less time for the completion of a round.

Golf is not all of life, but to have the opportunity to play outstandingly beautiful and ability-testing courses throughout the world is enriching life for an increasing number of people.

GOLF CLUBS

A player is permitted to carry a maximum of fourteen clubs to play golf. All golfers do not use a full set, and those using a full set do not all select the same clubs. However, the usual set of fourteen clubs consists of one putter, nine irons, and four woods. (see Ch. 10 Selection of Equipment and Accessories)

Putter

This club has an almost vertical clubface and has a relatively short shaft. It is used principally on the putting green (and near the green) to stroke and roll the ball into the hole. The design and construction of putters vary greatly: the shaft may be attached to any part of the clubhead; the size and contour of the grip may be different from the standard grip of the woods and irons; and the clubhead may be made in a variety of shapes.

Irons

Matched set of irons consist of eight or nine clubs: the eight-club set, 3-iron through 9-iron and wedge; the nine-club set, 2-iron through 9-iron and wedge. Due to the differences in shaft lengths and clubface lofts, the distances and trajectories of shots hit with the irons vary considerably. The distance differential between each of the irons is approximately ten yards. For instance, if you can

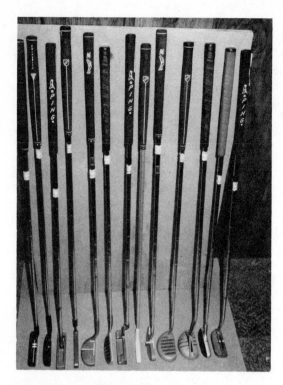

Fig. 1.3. Types of putters

hit a ball 130 yards with a 5-iron, you then can figure that you should hit a 4-iron 140 yards, and a 6-iron 120 yards.

The wedge has a heavier head and greater loft than the 9-iron. The club may be a pitching, sand, or dual purpose wedge. Some matched sets contain both a pitching and a sand wedge.

Besides the wedges, other special irons are made for hitting the ball short distances. Irons with medium loft and relatively short shafts are used to play low trajectory shots (run-up or chip shots) to the putting green. These clubs are marketed under various names but are generally called chipping irons.

In the past, irons were referred to by name, as for example: 2-iron, mid-iron; 5-iron, mashie; 9-iron, niblick. Today you will seldom hear any numbered iron called by name.

Woods

Matched sets of woods are usually made up of four clubs, numbers 1, 3, 4, and 5. Formerly, the 2-wood was included in all sets, but because of its limited usefulness it has declined in popularity. The shafts of the woods are longer than those of the irons, so that you can expect to hit the ball farther with these clubs than with the irons. Like the irons, the different numbered woods vary in shaft length and clubface loft. The almost vertical face of the driver restricts its use

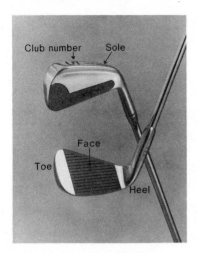

Fig. 1.4. Parts of clubhead

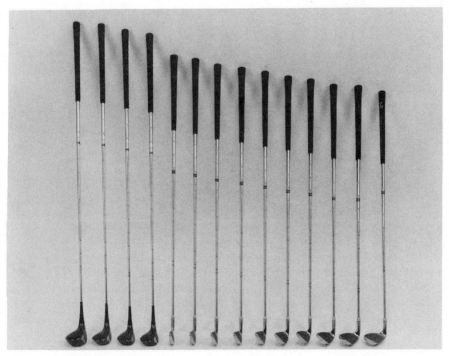

#1, 3, 4, 5, Woods   #2-9 Irons   Wedges
                                                Pitching and
                                                Sand

Fig. 1.5. Irons and woods

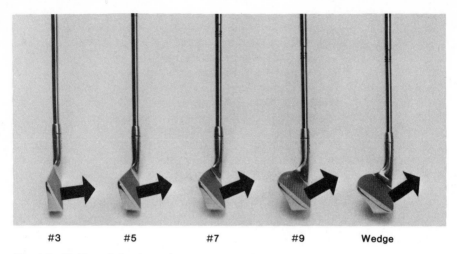

| #3 | #5 | #7 | #9 | Wedge |

Fig. 1.6. Clubface loft—irons

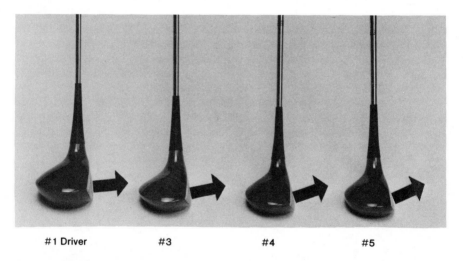

| #1 Driver | #3 | #4 | #5 |

Fig. 1.7. Clubface loft—woods

Photographs of irons and woods courtesy of Cobra Golf Inc.

to hitting the ball from a tee. The distance differential is approximately 10 yards between each of the different numbered woods. Some distinct changes have been made in the construction of the wood clubs. The clubheads may be made of other substances than wood, such as stainless steel, aluminum, or graphite. The degree of clubface loft may vary from an accepted standard to a slightly greater loft; thus, the club numbers are changed accordingly—from a 1-wood to a 1½wood, from a 3 to a 3½ wood, etc. Woods having a greater clubface loft than the 5-wood are gaining in favor as more are being manufactured. These higher-lofted woods are favored by players who prefer to hit wood shots rather than long iron shots.

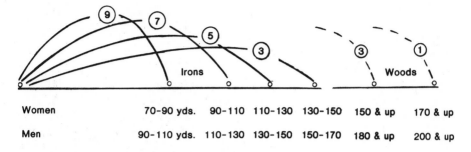

Fig. 1.8. Range of approximate distances—average
golfers

The 1-wood and the 3-wood are referred to by both name and number, driver, and spoon.

REVIEW QUESTIONS

1. What is par for men and for women on each of the following holes: 215 yards, 400, 170, 578, 600, 405, 470, and 256?
2. In an 18-hole handicap match one player is giving the opponent eleven strokes. As per score card illustrated, on what holes will strokes be given in a men's match? In a women's match? (See Ch. 10)
3. How important is the mental side of the game to the advanced player, the average player, and the novice? What part does the subconscious play in executing a golf shot?

safety—an important lesson

2

Golf is a relatively safe game, but if accidents occur they can be serious. Most accidents happen because players are careless or uninformed about safety practices. You have a *responsibility* for your safety and for the safety of others. Learn the following rules and *never take chances where safety is concerned.*

General Rules

1. Follow all precautions given to you by your instructor.
2. Before you swing a wood or an iron club, make sure that no one is close to being within range of your swing.
3. When another player is about to swing, be careful where you stand or walk. Stay well out of range of any swing.
4. Even though no one is within range of your swing, never swing carelessly so that the follow-through is directed toward anyone. You could hit and propel a pebble, rock, or divot toward that person. Also, although it is not likely to happen, the club could break or slip out of your hands.

At the Practice Range

1. Stay in the designated tee area. Do not walk or step ahead of the tee line to retrieve tees or balls.
2. If someone is teaching you or you are coaching another player, stand opposite and facing that person. Never stand on the player's right or left side in the path of the club. (At a crowded driving range be especially careful. Usually there is not enough space between the tee markers for both a "coach" and a student.)

On the Course

1. Do not stand or walk ahead of a player who is about to take a stroke that may endanger you. Similarly, before you are about to hit a ball that could

possibly endanger someone, make certain that no one is standing or walking ahead of you.

2. Before playing any stroke, be sure the group ahead is well out of range of your intended shot.
3. Before playing a shot to the putting green, wait until the group ahead has left the green and is safely out of range. When your group completes play on the putting green, replace the flagstick and leave the green immediately. (see Etiquette—Putting Green)
4. If you hit a ball that is travelling toward someone and may endanger that person, immediately call "FORE!" loudly to fully alert the player. (This warning may enable the player to take cover; for instance, "ducking" to protect his head and eyes.)
5. At par-3 holes on some courses, it is an accepted practice to invite the following foursome to tee off when all members of your group have played their shots to the putting green. While this following group is teeing off, your foursome should stand off the back edge of the green, preferably to one side of the hole, and watch the oncoming shots. After the tee shots have been taken, your group will then proceed to putt out.
6. Upon reaching the putting green of any hole, place your golf clubs or cart on the side or back of the green nearest the next tee. NEVER place your clubs in front of the green—(a player in the following group may carelessly shoot as you walk to the front of the green to retrieve your clubs, thus you will be in a dangerous position, possibly in the direct line of a ball flying to the green.)
7. If an object such as a tree or boulder is in your desired line of play, try to hit a safe shot avoiding the obstruction. Do not endanger yourself by hitting a ball that could rebound from the obstacle and fly back toward you. (If necessary, warn your playing companions to be alert or to take cover should your ball hit the object and ricochet.)
8. A golf course is one of several locations which are extremely hazardous during lightning and thunderstorms. The best precaution to follow is to avoid playing when such storms occur. The USGA Rule Book contains a section entitled, "Protection of Persons Against Lightning," which all players should read and follow.

Use of a Motorized Cart

When using a motorized cart to ride around the course, drive with care and follow the course rules for operation of the vehicle.

1. No more than two people should occupy the cart, and only authorized players should operate it. Do not allow children to drive the vehicle.
2. Never step out of the cart while it is moving—remain seated and keep arms, legs, and feet inside the cart until it comes to a full stop.
3. Drive slowly on slopes. Drive straight up and straight down hillsides.
4. Drive slowly when turning and avoid making sharp turns.
5. Be especially careful when driving on wet areas. To avoid skidding, drive slowly. Do not suddenly apply brakes.
6. Set the brakes before you leave the cart.

Many sports people carry personal liability insurance for protection in case accidents happen. The protection offered by these policies may merit your investigation and consideration.

Make golf a safe game. Follow all safety precautions—*be considerate, be alert,* and *use common sense.*

REVIEW QUESTIONS

1. Name at least six safety precautions to be followed on the golf course.
2. The careless practice of leaving golf clubs or cart at the front of the green while putting out not only slows up play on the course, it can be dangerous. Why?
3. What are the safety precautions to be observed when driving a motorized cart on the course?

some basic concepts
3

Too often golfers want to know "how" to swing a golf club. They want to know the intricate details of the swing—the complex analysis of the movement. Even if such an analysis were possible, what then? A full golf swing takes about two seconds. In that time how much can you think about and translate into action? Fortunately, conscious messages do not have to be sent to all involved body parts at the correct split second to make a golf swing. If this were necessary, no one could swing a golf club successfully.

FOCUSING ON DETAILS CAN SLOW YOUR PROGESS

Questions on whether the swing is natural or unnatural are meaningless. People of all ages, even those with physical handicaps, have learned to swing a golf club well. Some people have difficulty in learning the golf swings, but the problem is not in the movement. Attempting to execute the "how" by performing many details of action is one of the chief causes of learning difficulties. Trying to think of and perform many parts of the swing in two seconds is impossible and frustrating.

Emphasizing even one detail while swinging may cause trouble. No one questions that the left arm remains fairly straight during a swing (putting excepted). When the cue, "straight left arm," is carried beyond easy extension to an incorrect *stiff* position, the motion of swinging is restricted. Overemphasizing any detail can become an error that limits or distorts the whole swing.

TRUST YOUR NATIVE ABILITY FOR COORDINATION

Purpose is an important factor in determining the form of a motion. Suppose you wish to throw a ball straight up into the air. Your arm swings up sharply and your weight shifts upward with the motion. This coordination occurs without thought. You neither think of swinging your arm up nor of shifting your weight upward. Rather, you think of throwing the ball straight up into the air—and you do it!

Concentrating on the objective of the golf stroke—striking the ball to a target by swinging the club in a circular pattern—can develop a good swing. Novices fear that they cannot learn all the details of the swing. A player asks: "How can I remember to do all those things?" The encouraging answer, of course, is that it is unnecessary to think of numerous details. You can place some trust in your body to supply and coordinate many particulars. When you consider the everyday motor skills you perform, it is evident that this wondrous talent for coordination works almost automatically.

SOME BASIC SWING CONCEPTS

Understanding certain mechanical principles of clubhead action is important. Yet, many players make the mistake of ignoring such information. Instead of directing their attention to the clubhead, they focus their thinking upon what to do with some body part: head, shoulder, hip, knee, ad infinitum. If a ball is hit poorly they may work on changing the movement of some body part, rather than examining the trouble source—clubface and ball contact. Simple concepts of *swing pattern, clubface and ball contact,* and *clubhead speed and distance* provide guideposts for swinging a golf club well and hitting good golf shots.

Swing Pattern

Having a correct mental image of the arc of the golf swing is fundamental. To register the total concept of the arc, the swing must be viewed from the front and from the side. The swing is a circular motion on an inclined plane. While the clubhead gradually travels upward it also travels around the body. The swing is three-dimensional. (fig. 3.1)

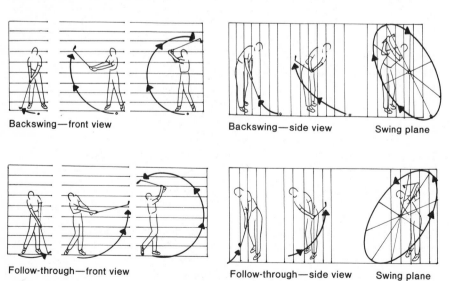

Backswing—front view   Backswing—side view   Swing plane

Follow-through—front view   Follow-through—side view   Swing plane

Fig. 3.1. Swing arc

The clubhead will follow a path of least resistance. The arc described by the clubhead may be a normal outcome of swinging the club to strike the ball from the ground to a distant target.

Having correct images of how the clubhead swings through the impact zone is also important. With relation to the ground level, *the clubhead travels close to the grass before and after ball contact.* With relation to the intended line of ball flight, *the clubhead enters the contact area from inside the line of flight, travels on the intended line of flight through the impact area,* and *on the follow-through travels inside the intended line of ball flight.* (fig. 3.2) This is the result of the clubhead travelling in an arc around you.

Fig. 3.2. Path of clubhead through contact area

Clubface and Ball Contact

The direction and flight of the ball can be directly related only to the contact of the clubface with the ball. Other factors may affect this contact, but they in themselves do not propel the ball—only the clubface can do that. If at ball contact the clubhead is travelling on the intended line of ball flight, and if the face is at right angles to that line, the ball will travel straight along the intended path to the target. These factors determine the direction the ball will travel: *the clubhead path through impact* and *the clubface position with relation to the clubhead path.*

A struggling golfer may say: "I can't get the ball up," or "I can't get under the ball." Until this person stops trying to propel the ball upward, his troubles will continue and probably increase. When a ball is hit properly, the slant of the clubface will determine the trajectory. No attempt should be made to hit the ball into the air. This understanding is basic to hitting good golf shots: *the clubface— not an effort on your part—will loft the ball into the air.*

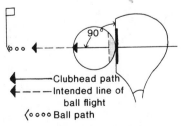

Fig. 3.3 Impact producing straight shot to target.

Golf requires a high degree of accuracy. A small error in club and ball contact may cause a great error in shot result. Considering the size of the golf ball and the small hitting surface of the clubface, it is a wonder that so many fine golf shots are made.

Clubhead Speed and Distance

One distinguishing characteristic of a fine golf swing is the smooth flowing acceleration of the clubhead. Drill on this quality of the swing seems to be neglected by many players, but not by the expert golfers. The experts "tune" their swings to smoothness, ease, tempo, and rhythm. Their objective is to develop one swing that they can trust to repeat—*and repeat*. This one smooth, accelerating swing produces great speed and distance, sometimes a greater distance than the player expected. This is a surprising and especially pleasant happening. But it is a "happening"—and wise players know this. Their practice has paid off and will continue to do so—they are on the right track.

Experimentation is the downfall of many players in their quest for long distance shots. They simply never get down to working on one swing and trusting that swing. Their swings are in a continual state of flux. These players would do well to follow the practices of fine golfers—to have the patience to work on developing one well-timed swinging motion; and, to permit, not force, clubhead speed to develop, and thus distance.

A typical mistake of many players is trying to swing faster or "harder" with certain clubs. For instance, after practice in hitting 7-iron shots a player changes to hitting 5-iron shots. Knowing that the ball should travel about 20 yards farther, a player may instinctively try to "add something" to the swing in order to get more distance. This is a mistake. The longer club, with less clubface loft, will produce the added distance.

Through intelligent practice you learn what the optimum speed is for swinging a golf club. The timing and smooth blending of forces that come with correct muscular action, together with the size of the arc, produce clubhead speed and distance, with accuracy.

LEARNING BY IMITATION

Imitation can be either an aid or a hindrance to learning. Young people imitate easily and to a high degree. Unlike some adults, they do not imitate on the intellectual or analytical level, but rather on a "subconscious" level. They grasp the *movement as a whole*. Pictures and feelings are registered, but not in words. Many caddies and young people have imitated fine golf swings, and this has played a part in their becoming good golfers.

When players try to copy minor swing details, swing styles, mannerisms, or idiosyncracies, they usually end up with what they copied—worthless details, not a better golf stroke.

In your imaginative brain center you probably have a picture of a golf swing accompanied by a feeling for the stroke. This may be a copy of one swing or an impression that has evolved from seeing many golf swings. If the picture is of a whole swing in good form, and the feeling is one of ease and good timing, then this mental image can be an aid in swinging the golf club well.

PROGRESSION IN LEARNING THE SWINGS

Skillful golfers prepare to play a round of golf by starting their practice using the medium or short irons. They hit shots requiring less than the full swing and then work to the longer swings and the longer clubs. This makes sense. The short swing is an important stroke of the game. The feel and touch for all golf swings are best found and recovered in these short strokes. Short swings serve as easy muscle and joint "warm-up" for the full swing.

The foregoing statements may be used to support this opinion: *if* it is best to start learning golf with a particular swing, then the choice should be the small swing. It is not suggested that the beginner delay working on the longer swings, but patience is recommended—walk before you run. More success in striking the ball can be expected with the less complex short swing than with the full swing. Success in striking the ball makes learning and practice more enjoyable as well as more effective. The putting stroke can be learned and practiced right along with the other strokes.

THE REAL SECRET

Useful guides can be given for learning golf and executing the swings, but no exact formula can be proposed. Who can confidently say he or she has all the answers to learning golf or to consistently hitting fine golf shots? Novices watch champions, note a detail of the swing, and think they have "discovered the secret" of good golf. Of one thing you can be sure—the champion does not want to know this *secret!* The champion already knows the REAL SECRET:—*following the fundamentals of good form in the grip, stance, and swing—and hitting thousands of golf balls in practice and play.*

You will become proficient in swinging a golf club as you have become proficient in other motor skills—through repetition. Through trial and error and, through trial and success, you will discard unsuccessful swing actions and record successful swings in your "muscle memory," and in your subconscious. You can develop an effective golf swing only by following the basics of good form and swinging a club many times.

REVIEW QUESTIONS

1. What are the advantages of starting practice with the short swings and progressing to the full swing?
2. Describe the correct clubhead path—before, at, and after impact—in relation to the intended line of ball flight and in relation to the ground level.
3. How much can you or should you think of when executing a golf shot?
4. What are your basic concepts on swinging a golf club?

addressing the ball
4

Taking the correct grip and the proper stance are essential preliminary steps in executing successful golf shots with the irons and woods. Some shots may be hit well when it appears that the fundamentals of grip and stance are defied, but neglect of the fundamentals only serves to tear apart a swing, because compensations must be made *constantly* to counteract the incorrect positions. Your best chance of developing a sound swing and game is to *start with the correct grip and stance.*

THE GRIP

Types of Grips

The *overlapping grip* is most widely used. In this grip, the little finger of the right hand rests on or overlaps the index finger of the left hand. In the *interlocking grip* the little finger of the right hand and the index finger of the left hand interlock. An advantage of either of these two positions is that there is a feeling of unity between the hands because of the overlapping or interlocking of the fingers. An advantage claimed for the overlapping grip is that both index fingers are on the shaft. Index fingers and thumbs are key components in holding anything. A person with small hands and short fingers may prefer the interlocking grip. Various names have been given the grip in which all the fingers of both hands are placed on the club. One claim made for this grip is that it is a strong one. The person who lacks grip strength or who has small hands may find the *10-finger grip* most suitable. Individual preference, feel, strength, and size of hands may all be factors in choosing the best grip for you.

The three grip positions are much alike: the only difference between them is the placement of the little finger of the right hand and the index finger of the left hand. All three grips have been used successfully; however, the overlapping grip is favored by the majority of golfers.

Overlapping   Interlocking   "10-finger"

Fig. 4.1. Types of grips

Steps in Taking the Grip (see Grip-Guide pattern, end of Ch. 4)

Left Hand
1. Place the club sole flat on the ground and support the tip of the handle with your right hand.
2. Let your left hand hang at your side. Feel the easy hanging position of the left hand and arm.
3. Without changing the natural hanging position of the left hand, move it forward to the club so that the club handle extends across the middle section of the index finger and back across the palm near the base of the little finger. (fig. 4.2) The hand, arm, and shoulder should still be in an easy, relaxed position. The back of the left hand faces the direction of the intended target. (Avoid the common error of gripping "under" the handle with the palm facing skyward.)
4. Keeping the left hand in this proper position and relaxed, close the fingers and take hold of the club handle (fig. 4.3). Hold the club with some firmness, but without tension. Holding the club with the left hand, you should be able to move the clubhead easily. (Try moving the clubhead just a few inches back and forth on the ground while maintaining this correct grip.)

Fig. 4.2.   Fig. 4.3.

Right Hand

1. Let the right arm hang easily at your side. Note its natural hanging position.
2. Without changing the easy hanging position of the right hand, move the hand to the club so that the club handle lies across the middle part of the index finger. The life line of the right palm is superimposed over the left thumb (fig. 4.4).

The palm of the right hand faces the direction of the intended target. The palms of the hands face each other. The right hand, arm, and shoulder should still be in an easy position.

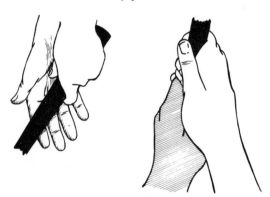

Fig. 4.4.   Fig. 4.5.

3. Close the fingers and palm of the right hand and take hold of the club. (fig. 4.5) In taking the overlapping grip, allow the little finger of the right hand to fall naturally over the index finger of the left hand. For the interlocking position, raise the index finger of the left hand and interlock it with the little finger of the right hand. It is important that the hand positions are not changed when the fingers are overlapped or interlocked.
4. Check the face of the club to see that it is *square* to the intended line of ball flight. (Check the firmness of the grip and ease of motion by moving the clubhead a few inches back and forth along the ground.)

Check Points—Left Hand

Take hold of the club, look down at your grip, and check the following numbered points (fig. 4.6).

1. The V formed by the thumb and index finger points to the general area between the chin and the right shoulder. Checking where the V points is a matter of judgment. Follow your instructor's specific instructions.
2. The base segment of the thumb will touch the side of the hand, forming a line.
3. The left thumb is slightly to the right of a center line along the shaft.
4. The knuckles at the base of the first two fingers can be seen, and perhaps the knuckle at the base of the third finger.
5. The tip of the thumb and tip of the index finger will lie close to each other.

Fig. 4.6. Left-hand grip   Fig. 4.7. Complete grip

Check Points—Right Hand (fig. 4.7)

1. The V formed by the thumb and index finger points to the general area between the chin and right shoulder. (See left hand grip.)
2. The base segment of the thumb will touch the side of the hand, forming a line.
3. The thumb is placed slightly to the left of a center line along the shaft.
4. The knuckle at the base of the index finger can be seen, and perhaps also the knuckle at the base of the long finger.
5. The tip of the thumb and the tip of the index finger lie close to each other. The tip of the thumb does not extend down the shaft beyond the middle segment of the index finger.
6. The left thumb fits in the life line of the right palm.

The hands send and receive messages about the swing. They are the sensory controls. They coordinate. In an effective hold on the club, they feel like a single unit—working together, neither one overpowering the other. The left-hand grip is more of a finger and palm grip, while the right is mainly a finger grip. The club must be held with authority, but this authority is for swinging the club, not for crushing the shaft! A vise-like, tenacious grip usually radiates tension up through the forearms, arms, and shoulders, thus preventing a free swing. The hold on the club must be firm, yet with a degree of ease and comfort, and remain that way throughout the swing.

Some players believe that wearing a glove on the left hand or gloves on both hands give them a better feeling of holding the club. (Wearing gloves may provide some protection for the fingers and hands. Players unaccustomed to swinging a club or engaged in extensive practice may tend to develop sore hands and blisters.)

Relation of Hand Position to Directional Ball Flight

The position of the hands on the club affects the directional flight of the ball. For instance, if the right hand is placed on the club so that the palm points skyward, the ball is likely to travel to the left of the target. The reason for this can be easily demonstrated. Grip the club with the right hand with the palm facing skyward and the clubface square to the intended target. Keeping the same hold on the club, turn the right hand so the palm faces the intended line of ball flight. Note that the clubface turns over and is in a closed position pointing to the left and downward. If either or both hands are placed on the club contrary to the easy hanging position, there will be a tendency for the hand or hands to return to the natural position during the swing, thereby changing the face of the club. (see Ch. 9, fig. 9.10)

Hand position will not always determine the directional flight of the ball because various compensations and efforts may be made during the swing to affect the clubface position.

Changing the grip to alter the ball flight is for the advanced player. When the hands are shifted to the left, the shot is likely to travel right; a shift of the hands to the right is likely to cause the ball to travel to the left. Changing the grip from the correct to the incorrect to eliminate errors in ball flight is not recommended. A balanced grip, as though "shaking hands" with the club handle and the palms in opposition to each other, is a basic key for taking the correct hold on the club.

THE STANCE

Types of Stances

Stances are classified by drawing a relationship between the intended line of ball direction and an imaginary line extending across the front edge of the toes. These two lines are parallel in the *square stance*, the one most widely used. Taking a stance with the lines across the toes, hips, and shoulders parallel to the target line is a natural position to assume.

If the stance is changed to an *open* or *closed* one for certain shots, the change should be slight. A square stance is recommended for most golf shots.

Stances vary in width for a logical reason—the width of the stance should fit the purpose of the swing. To hit a ball a long distance, the feet are placed approximately shoulder width apart. This stance will allow you to swing the club in a wide arc and to keep your balance while swinging the clubhead swiftly. To

Square   Closed   Open

Fig. 4.8. Types of stances

hit the ball a short distance, take a narrow stance. The same principle applies to the distance you stand from the ball. For distance shots, using the longer-shafted clubs, you will necessarily stand farther from the ball than for the shorter distance shots.

Steps in Taking the Stance

1. Sight and draw an imaginary line through the ball to the target.
2. Visualize the desired shot.
3. Holding the club correctly, place the club sole flat on the ground back of the ball as you sight again to see that the clubface is pointing toward the target. The edge of the clubhead where the sole and face meet should be perpendicular to the intended line of ball flight. (Step 1, fig. 4.9, 4.10) (The proper distance from the ball is established when the clubhead is placed back of the ball. The easily extended arms and the length of the shaft determine this distance. Avoid crowding the ball or stretching to reach it.)
4. Move the feet into the proper stance. (Step 2, fig. 4.9, 4.10)
   —For the short approach shot, take a comfortable, narrow stance. (A slightly open stance may be preferred over the square stance.)
   —For long shots take a comfortable stance with the feet about shoulder width apart.

The position of the ball in relation to the feet may vary slightly. For most long shots the unanimous recommendation is to play the ball approximately op-

Step 1   Step 2

Fig. 4.9. Taking stance for short approach shot.

Step 1   Step 2

Fig. 4.10. Taking stance for wood shot.

posite a point inside the left heel. For shorter shots the ball may be played from near this spot to a point extending toward the center of the stance.

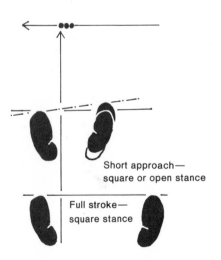

Short approach—
square or open stance

Full stroke—
square stance

Fig. 4.11. Stance and ball position relationship

Wood shot   Short iron shot

Fig. 4.12. Addressing the ball—side view.

Check Points—The Stance

1. The left arm and club shaft are approximately in a straight line. The arms hang easily from the shoulders—they are not held stiff. The right shoulder will naturally be slightly lower than the left because the right hand is placed lower on the grip.
2. The hands may be either slightly ahead of or above the ball. When looking down on the hands, it may appear that they are in a position left of the club-head.
3. The toes are turned out slightly. Turning the left foot out slightly more than the right may afford a freer swing through the ball. The knees are slightly bent—"easy" and ready to move.
4. The body is bent slightly forward from the hip joints and the back is fairly straight, but not rigid.
5. In the square stance the imaginary lines running across the shoulders, hips, and front tips of the shoes are parallel to the intended line of flight.
6. For long shots the feet are about shoulder width apart and the ball is opposite a point inside of the left heel. For the short shots the stance is narrow and the ball is opposite a point extending from the inside of the left heel toward the center of the stance.

Make the steps in addressing the ball simple and concise. When you know how to hold the club properly and how to take the correct stance, avoid making a "production" of addressing the ball. The simpler the process the better. You can place trust in your senses to aim correctly and to settle in a stance that is good for you.

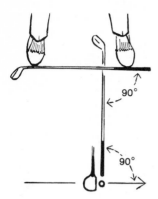

Fig. 4.13. Checking alignment with golf clubs.

THE WAGGLE AND FORWARD PRESS

A waggle is a movement of the *clubhead* in preparation for swinging the club—a rehearsal for starting the backswing. After the stance is taken the clubhead is moved away from the ball a short distance in the correct backswing path. Then it is moved forward to the ball and back to the address position. This gives you a "feel" of the club and a feeling of ease and confidence for starting the swing. The action of picking the club up and setting it down is not a waggle. Such nervous actions should be avoided.

A forward press is a movement of the body in preparation for beginning the swing. Just before the swing is started there is a slight "rocking" of weight to the left leg, accompanied by a slight bend of the right knee toward the left. Thus the name of the action—a press forward. Some golfers find that this slight shift forward helps them start the swing. Other players of varying skill do not use a forward press, or if they do the movement is so subtle that it can be scarcely seen.

The waggle and the forward press are not necessary actions, but rather auxiliary ones.

PRACTICE SUGGESTIONS

● Practice taking the grip. Place your hands on the club, check the grip, then release your hold on the club. Repeat this action until the correct grip becomes routine. By applying the check points and using the GRIP-GUIDE you can be confident that you will take and maintain a correct hold on the club. It will be easier to make any necessary adjustments of the grip, if first you take an easy, instead of a firm, hold on the club. Firm up the grip only after making sure it is correct.

● In your early practice of taking the grip, follow the steps in the text: (a) place the left hand on the grip and check the hand position; (b) then place the right hand on the club and check the complete grip. The grip will become comfortable and easy with practice. After practice in taking the grip in two steps, take the grip almost simultaneously with both hands. Have a feeling of the hands fitting together on the handle so they can work as a unit in swinging the club.

● Holding the club correctly, practice moving the clubhead in various patterns such as circles and figure 8's. (fig. 9.2) These exercises are a good test of the grip in action. The wrists and arms must be relaxed and flexible while the correct hold on the club is maintained. Note that as you direct your attention to moving the clubhead, the wrists and arms move—a responsive action.

● Some simple exercises can help you develop grip and arm strength: squeeze a soft sponge ball or towel; flex and extend the fingers and arms, offering your own resistance. Strength is developed by gradually increasing the number of movements you can make in a given amount of time.

● Address the ball and check the address position. As you do so, "let go," especially through the shoulders so that you will be relaxed and ready to move. Maintain a correct and firm grip.

● Practice taking the stance to different targets. Check to see whether the stance is square by laying a club on the ground with the shaft touching the front tips of your shoes. Then step back of the ball and see whether the club shaft is parallel with the intended line of flight. (fig. 4.13)

● Practice maintaining the correct body posture during the swing with this simple exercise. (fig. 9.4b) Without holding a club, assume an easy, comfortable stance. Check: feet shoulder width apart, knees "easy," and arms hanging free of the body. Swing arms back and forth. Watch a spot on the ground to maintain a fairly steady head position. Let the body and legs "give" with the swing. Gradually increase the arm swing to a point where the shoulders alternately move under the chin. Maintain the feel of the correct body posture throughout the swing.

REVIEW QUESTIONS

1. Even though it is possible to hit good shots despite faults in the grip and stance, why is it important to make sure these positions are correct?
2. List the points by which you can check your grip on the club.
3. What steps should be taken in assuming the stance for a golf shot?
4. How does the position of addressing the ball differ for an 8-iron, a 5-iron, and a 1-wood?

GRIP-GUIDE

How to Place GRIP-GUIDE Pattern on Club Handle

1 Set the sole of a medium iron flat on the ground, clubface pointing to the target.

②Mark a line down the center front of the club grip.

③Follow outlining broken lines and cut out rectangular form of Grip-Guide. (Grip-Guide patterns follow, page 30)

④Place notches of Grip-Guide on center line of club handle and tape onto club.

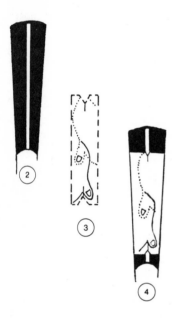

How to Place Hands on Grip-Guide Pattern

The key to the correct hold on the club is placing the thumb and index finger of each hand on the pattern—top hand on dotted line and lower hand on solid line. With the positions of the thumbs and index fingers correct, the remaining fingers, as they are wrapped around the handle, will normally assume their proper positions.

1. *Top hand*—place thumb and index finger on dotted line and take hold of the club. Edge of index finger should fall on or near the dotted line indicated, forming a V between thumb and index finger.

Check Points for Top Hand:
  a. Thumb slightly to side of center line.
  b. V between thumb and index finger points in general direction of right shoulder. (Left-handers, left shoulder)
  c. As you look down on the grip, the knuckles at base of first two fingers (and possibly third finger) can be seen.
  d. Tip of thumb and lower edge of index finger are in a position approximately equidistant down the club handle.

  2. *Lower hand*—place thumb and index finger in position on solid line. (Note V between thumb and edge of index finger). Wrap all fingers, except little finger, around handle. For the OVERLAPPING grip, let little finger overlap index finger of top hand; INTERLOCKING, interlock little finger and index finger of top hand; TEN-FINGER, wrap little finger with others around club.

Check Points for Lower Hand:
  a. Thumb is slightly to side of center line.
  b. V between thumb and index finger points in general direction of right shoulder. (Left-handers, left shoulder)
  c. As you look down on the grip, the knuckle at base of index finger (and possibly long finger) can be seen.
  d. Tip of thumb and lower edge of index finger are in a position approximately equidistant down the handle.
  e. Palms of hands should face each other.

Adjustments

For extremely large or small hands, place the thumbs and index fingers in the same relative position that the Grip-Guide indicates, but outside or inside the guide lines. In most cases little or no adjustment will be necessary.

After placing the hands on the Grip-Guide in their proper positions, very slight adjustments may be made for greater ease in holding the club, but do not fail to keep thumb and index fingers close to pattern.

Safety Precautions

After Grip-Guide is taped firmly in place, practice taking the grip. When you feel you are holding the club securely and there is no danger of the club slipping out of your hands, practice taking the small swings and progress to the longer swings.

Grip-Guide should help you learn the correct grip. When you feel confident that you can hold the club properly, discontinue using the Guide. It has then served its purpose.

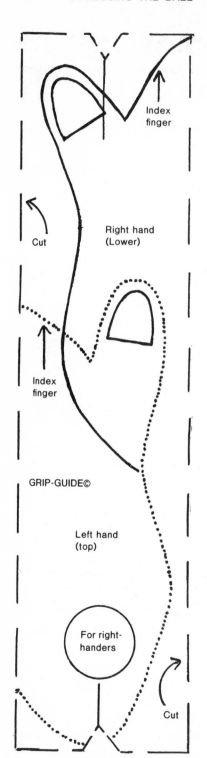

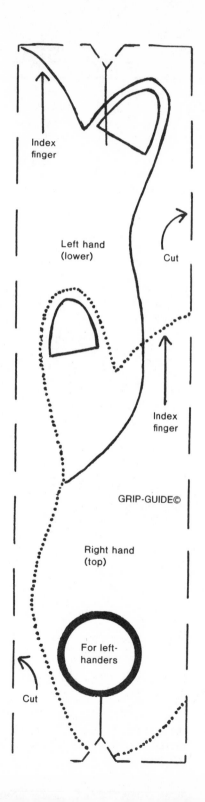

short approach shots
5

The short approach shots played to the putting green are *pitch shots* and *chip* (*or run-up*) *shots.* The pitch shot is played with a high-lofted iron, thus the ball travels in a high trajectory and upon landing tends to stop with little or no forward roll. When a ball is contacted squarely with a lofted iron, the clubface will compress the ball well below its center of gravity, thus imparting backspin to it. This backspin and the height from which the ball falls to the ground will tend to stop the forward motion of the ball when it lands. In some instances the ball will bounce backwards after landing.

The chip or run-up shot is usually stroked with a medium iron. The ball travels in a relatively low trajectory. The chip shot will, after landing, roll a longer distance than a typical pitch shot, due to the lack of backspin and to the low trajectory.

Approach shots vary greatly in length, from perhaps gently stroking a ball a distance of 20 feet or less, to hitting shots of about 100 yards. These strokes plus the putting stroke, the *short game,* make up a substantial percentage of the shots a player takes in a round of golf.

The terms *one-quarter, one-half,* and *three-quarter* are often used to describe the approximate lengths of the swings. Through practice you learn how far to swing the club in order to hit the ball a given distance. You sight and judge the distance for a shot, and then through the remarkable sense of "feel" (kinesthetic sense) you swing the club the distance your eye, feel, and experience dictate. One subconsciously translates the synthesis of judgments into the execution of the golf shot. At times all golfers experience the thrill of stroking approach shots expertly, either by having the ball come to rest inches from the hole or by holing the shot.

CHIP SHOT

Consider the following situations for playing a chip shot: one ball lies 50 feet from the hole and about 5 feet off the putting green; the other lies 20 feet from the hole and 3 feet off the putting surface. (fig. 5.1A, B) The fringe grass is heavy, therefore rolling a putt through the area is questionable. The better shot, under

31

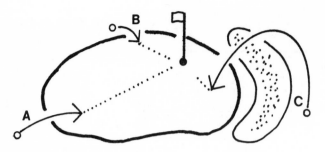

Fig. 5.1. Approach shots

these conditions, is a chip shot. The ball is played to carry over the heavy apron grass, land on the green, and roll toward the cup. For the longer shot, any of the medium irons, 4-iron through 7-iron, is suitable. The best club to use for the shorter distance, where a limited roll is necessary after the ball lands on the green, is a high-lofted iron.

The swing to visualize is pendulum-like, with the clubhead swinging close to the ground and on or close to the intended target line. (fig. 5.2) With a smooth swinging motion, a consistent and correct clubhead path can be expected. If, however, the club is lifted, or jerked during the swing, neither consistency nor accuracy is possible.

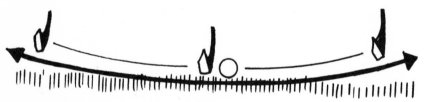

Fig. 5.2. Clubhead path—pendulum-like swing

A feeling for the stroke and the distance can be "rehearsed" by swinging the "throwing" hand and arm (without a club) in an underhand motion as though tossing a ball to land on the green and roll to the cup. After swinging the arm, hold the hands together in a golf grip and take the same underhand swing. Then try the same motion holding the club. Feel the hands swinging together as one unit. The hands and arms swing freely as the clubhead sweeps the grass.

For accuracy and the feel and touch for stroking the ball a short distance, grip down ("choke up") on the handle and take a narrow, comfortable stance with the knees bent easily. Some players prefer to take a slightly open stance with slightly more weight carried to the left side. They believe these adjustments help establish a feel for a small swing. Also, they feel that the open stance allows a better view of the target. Whether the stance is square or slightly open, it must be comfortable and easy.

No extra effort is made to hit the ball or loft it into the air.

Fig. 5.3. Approximate one-quarter swing

PITCH SHOT

A typical pitch shot situation is one in which the ball lies about 30 to 40 yards from the hole and a deep bunker intervenes between the ball and the green. (fig. 5.1C) The ball must be stroked with a high-lofted iron, such as a wedge or 9-iron, so it will carry over the bunker, land on the green, and take relatively little forward roll. The stroke for the pitch shot is a swinging motion, as it is for the chip shot. A smooth, even swing can be "grooved" to produce consistently good shots.

For a given distance a pitch shot must be hit with more force (clubhead speed) than a chip shot. Some distance is taken off the pitch shot due to the higher ball flight. On the longer swing for the pitch shots (and the chip shots) the clubhead will naturally swing inside the target line and then upward on the backswing and on the follow-through. Through the impact area the clubhead travels on the target line and close to the ground. Some changes in addressing the ball will accommodate the longer shots: a longer hold on the club handle will produce more clubhead speed; a wider stance, square and balanced, will allow a freer and fuller swing.

Fig. 5.4. Half swing

For approach shots it is difficult to pinpoint an exact spot where the ball should be played in relation to the stance. In certain approach shots some players prefer to play the ball opposite a point near the right foot. Through practice and experience you will find the ideal position for stroking the ball, which will probably be in the area opposite the center of the stance and extending to a point opposite the inside of the left foot.

Sometimes it is desirable to hit a ball in a higher or lower trajectory than normal for a specific club. A change in the position from which the ball is played may alter the flight of the ball. A ball played more to the left side of the stance will tend to travel in a higher trajectory; one played more toward the right foot, in a lower trajectory.

STROKE EXECUTION—SOME ANALYSIS AND DETAIL

The details of the swing may be the result of having the correct grip and stance, and swinging the clubhead with the correct purpose in mind.

● The clubhead is swung in an arc, keeping the same radius throughout the swing. *Result*—the left arm will maintain the easy extended position it assumed in addressing the ball.

- During the swing there is a lack of tension in the shoulders and arms. *Result*—there is a free arm and shoulder motion in the swing.
- The grip is correct and firm but not tense. *Result*—there will be a gradual bending of the wrists if the clubhead is swung. If the handle of the club is carried back and forth or if it is lifted, there can be no normal responsive action of the wrists. The cooperative action of the wrists becomes more apparent as the swing lengthens. Wrist action is a gradual motion. It does not occur at a certain spot. No conscious effort should be made to "use" the wrists.
- As the swing begins, the stance is comfortable and the knees are bent slightly. *Result*—there may be a slight give of the body in the direction of the swing, but not a "give" of the head. As the club is swung back the left knee will naturally give to the right side, and there will be a tendency for a slight weight shift to the right foot. On the forward swing the opposite action occurs. Like the wrist motion, this action of the body and legs becomes greater and more evident as the swing lengthens.

There is a fusion of all details into one unit of motion. Good form can develop as a result of swinging the clubhead.

Grip, Hand Action, and Wrist Action

If the hold on the club is changed during the swing, an awkward action of the hands and wrists is almost certain to occur. A check on the positions of the hands can be made at any point in the swing. Swing the club to a point where you wish to look at the grip, then stop the swing. Turn your head so that you are looking at the hands from the same angle as you observed them in addressing the ball. The grip should be the same as at address.

A common fault in making the swing for the short approach shot is attempting to scoop the ball up into the air. In this erroneous action the hands, instead of working together, work in opposition to each other. Near ball impact the right hand moves forward and under, as the left hand holds back. A common outcome of this error is striking the ground with the clubhead before striking the ball. Through the impact area both hands must move with the clubhead. At times there may be a feeling that the hands are leading the clubhead. (see Ch. 9, fig. 9.6)

The wrist action that occurs in a swing can be easily checked and rehearsed. Keeping the arms extended as in the address position, raise the clubhead and point it forward and then over your right shoulder. (fig.5.5) When pointing the clubhead over the shoulder, keep the left elbow easily extended and let the right elbow bend. Note that if the club handle is lifted with the hands and arms, there will be no bending of the wrists.

Knee Action and Foot Action

Action of the knees, feet, and legs is a part of swinging the clubhead in a certain direction. Because of previously developed muscle habits and tension there might be a lack of response in developing this combined action. Rather than complicating the swing by thinking of how to move your feet or which foot to move,

Fig. 5.5. Wrist action exercises

this part of the swing can be practiced by itself without breaking up the blending action of all parts of the swing. A simple practice exercise is to alternate bending the left knee toward a spot in front of the right foot, and then bending the right knee so that it points to a spot in front of the left foot. Accompanying this knee bending is some inward action of the ankle and foot. The weight shifts to the inner border of the foot and big toe. The heel may rise slightly from the ground with the inner border rising less than the outer border. When your muscles have been trained to move in this manner and have developed a "feeling" for the motion, then you can expect to move the legs and feet correctly when you swing the club. This practice exercise plus the directional influence of the swing will help develop a correct and natural action. (fig. 5.6)

Fig. 5.6. Foot and leg action exercise

Head Position

In all golf swings the head remains in a fairly stationary position until after the ball is struck. After ball contact, the head will turn naturally to accommodate the follow-through of the swing. There should be no question about this mechanical aspect of the swing.

The cue "watch the ball until you strike it" is useful for maintaining a steady head position during the swing. But the cue "keep your head down" can cause serious errors if the position is exaggerated. If the head is held "down" so that the chin is resting on or near the chest, the shoulders are prevented from alternately moving under the chin on the backswing and follow-through. Even though this incorrect head position may not be a problem on very small swings where there is limited shoulder action, it is a habit to be avoided. One other error that may result from the "head down" cue is moving the head down and lower during the backswing. This restricts the backswing. Also, because the head must be moved back up to the address position when the ball is struck, the control and momentum of the clubhead are destroyed.

SELECTING THE BEST APPROACH SHOT

When a ball lies close to the green, the best stroke to play may be putting the ball over the apron and onto the putting surface. If the intervening area between the ball and the edge of the green is relatively smooth and the ball will roll easily over the grass, choose to putt the ball rather than playing a chip shot. Using a putter from off the green (sometimes humorously referred to as a "Texas wedge") can often save strokes.

Situations Favoring the Chip Shot (Run-Up Shot)

If playing a putt from off the green has been ruled out, and there is no necessity for lofting the ball high into the air, a chip shot may be the logical stroke to play. For most golfers it is easier to judge how a ball will roll over the green after landing than to guess how a pitch shot will react upon hitting the green. Another consideration favoring the chip shot is that it usually requires a smaller swing (with less force) for a given distance. If an error is made, such as topping, the error in shot result is likely to be less than it would be with the stronger hit pitch shot.

If a high trajectory shot is not needed, a run-up shot (landing short of or on the putting green) is favored in the following situations:

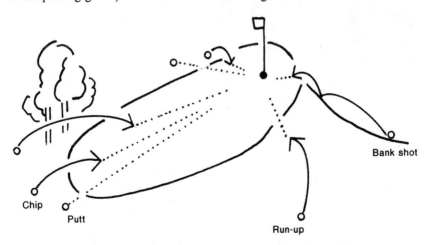

Fig. 5.7. Approach situations

- When the greens are dried out and hard and pitch shots will not "hold" on the green.
- If the ball is lying in a poor position, such as on sparse or bare ground. Usually it is less difficult to hit the ball from poor lies with medium-lofted irons.
- When playing in a strong wind. Hit low shots to avoid the wind effects.
- When it is necessary to hit the ball low, such as under the limbs of a tree.
- When an elevated area intervenes between the ball and the putting green, and there is insufficient space for landing the ball on the green ("little green to work with"). Hit a low run-up shot to strike the bank, rebound upward and onto the green ("bump-and-run" shot).

Situations Favoring the Pitch Shot

The pitch shot can be an effective stroke when the following conditions exist:

- The ball lies in a good position on the turf.
- The greens are relatively soft and will "hold" pitch shots.
- There is sufficient space on the putting green ("plenty of green to work with") for the ball to land and come to rest close to the hole.

For longer approach shots played under these conditions, the pitch shot played to the putting green is preferred over the run-up shot played to land short of the green. Sometimes, however, it is necessary to hit a pitch shot to land short of the green and then bounce forward onto the green (pitch-and-run). If the ball has to be lofted into the air and there is a sharp downhill roll to the cup (or if the cup is located close to the edge of the green) a pitch shot must be played to land on the apron—not on the putting surface. (In these situations, if a ball were played to the putting green, it would most likely roll well past the hole, possibly off of the green.)

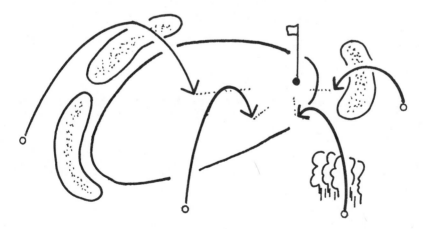

Fig. 5.8. Pitch shots

Today's players have become proficient in hitting pitch shots to the greens. The pitching wedge is favored for these shots, but good pitch shots can be made with the 9-iron or even the 8-iron. It is a mistake to try to hit the ball an extra long distance with a wedge. Hitting a pitch shot with a high-lofted iron may be a better shot to play than trying to "press" a wedge to the distance limit. Playing expert wedge shots takes a good deal of practice and experience—and ideal course conditions.

In playing approach shots or putts from off the green, the flagstick (pin) may be attended or removed from the cup, or left in the hole. If the ball is played from off the putting green, there is no penalty if it strikes the unattended flagstick. Most players prefer to have the pin left in the hole and unattended. Sometimes the stick will act as a backstop for a firmly hit or a downhill shot. The ball may fall into the hole or end up inches away from the cup if and when it strikes the flagstick.

PRACTICE SUGGESTIONS

● Picture the action of a playground swing—swinging back-and-forth, back-and-forth. Swing the clubhead in this rhythmic manner. Sweep the grass with each back-and-forth motion. The clubhead speed will be the same for the backswing and the forward swing. This continual motion creates certain details of form. The wrists "give" or bend, acting as hinges, allowing the clubhead to swing in a longer arc than the hands. The outward pull of the swing (centrifugal force) causes the left arm to swing in an extended position. The

ED FIORI, Member, Advisory Staff, Ben Hogan Golf Co.

body and legs give in the direction of the swing. Without striking a ball, practice one swing at a time. Watch the clubhead sweep the grass at the start of the swing and through the impact area. Hold the finish of the swing and feel control of the club with the hands.

● Hit many chip shots from near the green. Practice until you are machine-like in performance. Pick out a spot on the green where the ball should land, and visualize the desired shot. Aim to "sink" each shot. The shots failing to drop into the cup should stop very close to it.

● In changing from practicing chip shots to hitting pitch shots, you may sense a difference in the swings. For a given distance hitting a pitch shot with a higher-lofted iron will require a longer swing. More responsive wrist action occurs as the swing lengthens, so that a player may sense more wrist action in the pitch shot. The longer swing and the differences in clubhead weights and shaft lengths all contribute to what you feel about the stroke. This is a result. To deliberately try to develop two definite, different swings is neither necessary nor recommended.

● Work from short approaches to longer ones. Change the target both for distance and line of direction. Make mental notes on the different length shots such as how much to "choke up" on the grip, the width of the stance, and the necessary length of swing.

● Practice stroking the ball from good lies on the turf. When you are hitting the shots well, try hitting the ball from both good and fair lies. Stroking the ball from other than a good lie is not so much a matter of learning how to do it, but rather a matter of facing the situation without anxiety. Avoid practice from poor lies if you are hitting unsatisfactory shots. Such practice tends to destroy confidence and disrupt a good swing pattern.

● Reverse the club and grip the shaft near the clubhead with the end of the handle about six inches from the ground. Swing the tip of the handle back and forth continually. Then take the regular grip on the handle and swing the clubhead. After the continual swinging, practice taking one swing at a time. You will definitely feel the clubhead after swinging the comparatively weightless handle. For even greater sensitivity for the clubhead and the touch of hand control, take the same swings with the eyes closed.

● Stand with your feet together and take an approximate half-swing. This stance will require you to swing smoothly and in balance.

● Practice swinging in front of a mirror. Pay particular attention to the start of the swing and the clubhead arc.

Short strokes are an important part of your game. Spend the first part of every practice session on them.

REVIEW QUESTIONS

1. In all human motor skill performance many details of a motion occur without conscious thought directed to the detail. How can the movement of swinging a golf club produce correct details of good form? How can incorrect concepts of the swing affect details of good form?
2. If you are playing a shot from off the putting green, what are your options regarding the flagstick? How would such conditions as the terrain and the distance from the hole affect your choice of an option?
3. Under what conditions would you choose to hit a chip shot to the putting green? A putt? A pitch shot?

the full strokes—
irons and woods
6

Essentially, the swings taken to hit a wood shot and an iron shot are the same. That the swings may feel somewhat different is to be expected. There are differences in shaft lengths, club balances, club weights, swing speeds, and swing arcs. In the wood swing the path of the clubhead is closer and more level to the ground for a longer distance through the ball contact area than it is with the irons. The wood swing may feel more like a sweep than the swing with the irons. One often hears that in playing an iron there should be a feeling of hitting down on the ball. If exaggerated, this cue can lead to trouble. For some players, especially novices, the idea of "hitting down on the ball" may result in a poor swing and a poor shot. Whether hitting an iron or a wood shot, the prime objective is to *swing the clubhead to hit the ball out to a target.*

THE SWINGS

Playing the High-Lofted Irons

The higher-lofted irons are designed for a high degree of accuracy. A swing somewhat less than the full swing may be recommended for these clubs. This is sensible. There is less movement involved in a three-quarter swing than in a full swing, thus a greater chance of being accurate. This motion is an extension of the half swing. No great effort need be made to increase the swing. With a purpose of stroking the ball a slightly longer distance, a longer swing will naturally be taken. Some players use an approximate three-quarter swing for all the full iron shots and for the wood shots. (fig. 6.10)

A Look at the Full Swing and Some Analysis

Addressing the Ball (For a complete review, see Ch. 4)
- A definite target is chosen within the player's distance potential.
- The stance is comfortable. The feet are approximately shoulder width apart.

Fig. 6.1. Addressing the ball.   Fig. 6.2. Starting the backswing.

● The arms hang easily from the shoulders. The left arm and the club shaft are in an approximate straight line.

Starting the Swing
● The swing is started slowly and smoothly—with ease. No attempt is made to hurry, lift, or grab the club handle.
● The clubhead is swung back close to the ground. The hands, arms, and shoulders move as a unit accompanied by a natural "give" of the legs and body.
● The feeling is one of swinging the clubhead straight back away from the ball, but after a certain point the clubhead will normally swing inside the intended line of ball flight. Halfway into the backswing, the hands, and easily extended arms, and the clubhead will be approximately opposite the right side.

Top of the Swing
● The club shaft is approximately horizontal.
● The left arm is easily extended, maintaining the swing radius. The right elbow is bent and pointing down, and slightly away from the right side.
● The wrists are bent (cocked) and in a position approximately under the club handle.
● The shoulders and hips have turned. The left shoulder is about under the chin. To accommodate this body rotation, some weight has shifted to the right side, and the left leg and foot have responded in the direction of the swing. The left heel has risen slightly.

Fig. 6.3. Top of the swing

Fig. 6.4. Top of the swing—side view

Downswing

● No attempt is made to rush into the downswing—patience is a key thought. When the start of the downswing "feels" slow, it is apt to be correct.

● The downswing is a blended gathering of forces for contacting the ball with a swiftly moving clubhead. These actions merge one into the other.

—The left heel returns to its original position on the ground and the body weight begins to shift to the left side.

—The hips shift slightly to the left, and the body starts to turn in the direction of the swing.

Fig. 6.5. Downswing

Fig. 6.6. Downswing—side view

—The arms swing downward with the left arm remaining in its extended position and with the right elbow coming close to the side.
—The wrists remain in a cocked position reserving clubhead acceleration for a split second later.

Impact

● The body is in a firm position of balance, contributing to the clubhead attaining optimum speed at ball contact.
● The clubhead catches up with the hands. The hands, arms, and clubhead move through the impact area together.
● The head remains fairly still.

Follow-through

● Through the impact zone the clubhead swings close to the ground and on the intended line of ball flight, and then gradually moves inside that line and upward.
● The objective, swinging the club to hit the ball to a distant target, along with the swiftly moving clubhead, produces a follow-through in good form.
   —The shoulders and hips turn so the body is facing the intended target. Good balance is maintained.
   —The head turns and gradually rises to accommodate the full finish and to see the shot result.
   —The right knee bends and turns so that it is touching (or near) the left knee and pointing toward the target. The right heel is well off the ground.
   —The speed of the clubhead carries the arms up, with the hands finishing high and maintaining their hold on the club.

Fig. 6.7. Impact   Fig. 6.8.

Fig. 6.9. Follow-through

THE SEARCH FOR DISTANCE—CAUTIONS AND SUGGESTIONS

Progressing to the point of stroking the ball with the long irons and woods should not be a complicated step. The objective is to strike the ball to a more distant target, but a target within your distance potential. If the objective should become hitting the ball with all one's might, such complications arise as poor coordinations, muscle tensions, and poor timing. They are the curse of the beginner and experienced player alike.

Muscular Contraction and Relaxation

Some practical knowledge about muscle action can be helpful. Try this experiment related to using muscles effectively and ineffectively. Extend your right arm out in front of you with your palm facing up. Bend the elbow and touch your fingers to your shoulder. Now again extend the arm, but this time tightly tense, (contract) all the arm muscles. Keeping the muscles tense, try bending your elbow. This action is now difficult, if not impossible. Why? You are preventing muscles used in the motion from performing. When you relax—let go—they can perform easily. Tensing up when you want the arm to move is like stepping on a car's accelerator and brake at the same time.

When golfers try to hit the ball "hard" to get distance, they tend to use muscles that resist and even "block" the intended movement. Muscular contractions of resistance plus strong muscular contractions to overcome the resistance may make a swing feel powerful, but these contradictory efforts spell ruin for distance and accuracy. All players can be misled by the "feeling" of a golf swing. When a fine shot is hit a considerable distance, a player is apt to say: "But I swung so easy." That is true. The muscle action was synchronized: resistant actions were avoided and the right contractions were made. The swing felt "good."

KEITH FERGUS, Member, Advisory Staff, Wilson Sporting
Goods Co.

Fig. 6.10. Approximate three-quarter swing

PAT BRADLEY, Member, Advisory Staff, Dunlop Golf Co.

BETH STONE, Member, Advisory Staff, Ben Hogan Golf Co.

SAM SNEAD, Courtesy of Wilson Sporting Goods Co.

After hitting a beautiful long shot with an "easy" swing, you may theorize: "If I can hit that distance, why not 'put something into it' and get my full distance." But what can you put into the swing? If it is more clubhead speed, then a longer shot can be expected. But if you are misled into "muscling the ball" (adding tension) then you will probably hit the ball a shorter distance. When the swing feels easy and possibly slow, you may be swinging with the best possible clubhead speed.

Timing the Swing

If you can avoid "hurrying to hit" the ball, your chances for developing and maintaining well-timed swings are good. Speeding up the swing to hit the ball great distances destroys tempo and rhythm and produces poor and painful golf shots—so much is put into the motion and so little is gained. A well-timed swing produces accuracy and optimum speed at and through ball contact. Consider these suggestions to help time your swing:

- Since the swing is started from a motionless position, it must begin slowly and evenly. Then a gradual and smooth acceleration of the clubhead follows.
- The feet, legs, body, arms, and hands must work together, each supplying its own power. Arguing and trying to reach a decision on whether a particular body part plays a more important role in timing or in power is futile. The fact that you can move your hands and arms faster than you can move your body and legs furnishes a lead for timing. You cannot "flail away" with the hands and arms and have the legs and body trying to "catch up" by lunging and jerking. The arms and hands must be attuned to the speed at which the legs and body can move.
- Many players find that counting helps their swings. The backswing is counted as 1, the top of the swing 2, and the downswing 3; or, 1—and —2; or, back—and—through. Some players use only two counts; some use key words which have significance for them.
- Keeping the same tempo and rhythm for all strokes is recommended. Key your timing to a medium iron and maintain the same tempo when you progress to the long irons and woods. Many a player has ruined a golf game by keying his timing to fast swings with the driver. A player rushes to the golf course, takes a few strenuous swings with the driver, and hits a few practice shots as hard as he can. During the round this player is likely to say: "My timing is off today."

The synchronization of a fine golf swing that produces accurate and long golf shots is beyond human description, but within human achievement.

DISTANCES AND CLUB SELECTION

The Irons

The distance range between the shortest and the longest iron is approximately 100 yards. Sometimes, however, players fail to hit the ball the expected distance with the longer irons. The probable reason, other than lack of practice or experience, is expending useless effort to hit the ball farther. Longer clubs should yield longer shots. Some players tempted to hit the ball far, prevent the club from doing its job.

TSUNEYUKI NAKAJIMA, Member, Advisory Staff, Mizuno Golf Co.

AYAKO OKAMOTO, Member, Advisory Staff, Mizuno Golf
Co.

The amount of clubface loft of the irons ranges from about 20 to 50 degrees, hence the different ball flight trajectories. For any specific iron the flight trajectory may be changed by increasing or decreasing the clubface loft when addressing the ball. Increasing the loft, "opening the face," will produce a higher than normal shot; decreasing the loft, "closing the face," a lower than normal shot.

Through practice and experience you learn just how far you can hit the ball with each iron. If the distance to the green calls for a 5-iron shot, hit the ball with that club—do not "press" a 6-iron. To score well, always use "enough club."

The Woods

The driver, 1-wood, is designed to hit the ball from a tee—only in unusual circumstances is it used from the fairway. Some players who find the driver a "problem club" tee off with the 3-wood. Also, players choose to drive with a fairway wood (or a long iron) when the hole is an especially treacherous one— as when shooting onto a very narrow fairway bordered by an out of bounds on one side and deep rough on the other side. Sacrificing some yardage for a chance of being accurate and avoiding trouble is good playing strategy.

In playing wood shots from the fairway, the position of the ball on the ground is more important than any distance consideration in deciding what club should be used. The higher-lofted woods are more effective in hitting from fair and poor lies than is the 3-wood. For difficult and troublesome lies, even though the ball may be a wood distance from the hole, an iron shot will usually be the better shot to play.

PRACTICE SUGGESTIONS

● Take short and full swings without hitting a ball. To help increase left hand and arm strength, practice swinging while holding the club with only the left hand. To check for maintaining a steady head position, stand so that your shadow casts in front of you and watch your head's shadow.
● Practice the exercises for developing the footwork and body turn (pivot). (fig. 6.11 and 6.12)
● Use common sense when practicing.
　—Work from hitting short iron shots to the full shots. Warm up. Avoid beginning to practice by "whaling away at the ball" with the driver. Not only may muscle and joint strain occur, but such action can destroy a golf swing.
　—Avoid extra long practice sessions. Break up the practice times with rest periods.
　—When hitting iron shots from artificial turf or from hard ground, avoid trying to hit "down" on the ball or trying to take divots. The reverberation of the shock of hitting a hard surface could injure hands, wrists, arms, or shoulders.
● If the long iron and the wood shots are unsatisfactory, try hitting shots with a shorter hold on the club. After some success, gradually work up to the full hold.

Fig. 6.11.

Fig. 6.12.

- If it is difficult to hit balls off the grass (irons and woods), tee up the balls. Then return to hitting balls from good lies. With confidence restored, you can stroke the ball from varying positions without anxiety.
- Practice hitting the ball to different specific targets. Change both line of direction and distance. Learn the specific distances you can hit the ball with each club.

REVIEW QUESTIONS

1. What does timing a swing mean to you? How can a well-timed swing improve your golf shots? What are some points to remember in developing a swing of proper tempo and rhythm?
2. Can you make a reasonable estimate of how far you can strike the ball with each of your clubs?
3. Why is it important to swing with some ease rather than exert yourself to hit the ball hard? How can a feeling of "power" be misleading?

the putting stroke
7

If open putting tournaments were held—to include men and women, amateurs and professionals—it would be unwise to bet only on the professionals to win. Many average golfers are exceptionally skillful in putting. These experts have an outstanding "touch and feel" for the stroke; this is something they have learned and developed, but something that cannot be taught. Accompanying this quality is a confidence, a sureness that they are good putters. This confident demeanor and the sense of touch and feel cannot be separated—they almost become one and the same. Without one, the other is impossible.

Quietly accepting the idea that you can be a good putter paves the way for your becoming one. Players who seem to revel in declaring themselves poor putters usually remain so; avoid joining them!

The acceptance of a confident attitude nourishes concentration. With the mind free of doubt, it can focus its attention on the job to be done: in this case, putting the ball into the hole. A gentle and quiet mental preparation, without self-harrassment, can be the key to a successful putting game.

ADDRESSING THE BALL

Good putting requires a feeling of ease and a gentle seriousness for the stroke to be made. This attitude begins with taking a comfortable grip and stance.

The Hold on the Club

The reverse-overlapping grip is favored by the majority of golfers. The hands are placed on the handle with the palms approximately facing each other and with the thumbs down the front of the shaft. The index finger of the left hand overlaps the little finger of the right hand, or extends downward and overlaps more than one finger. No claim can be made that there is only one best grip. Players have become fine putters by holding the club in various ways and styles, such as the 10-finger grip; a cross-handed grip (hands in reverse position on the handle); and the right index finger extended down the right side of the club handle.

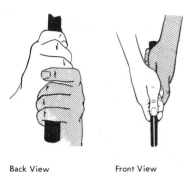

Back View   Front View

Fig. 7.1. Reverse-overlapping grip

Fig. 7.2. Putting stance

The Stance

Just as there is no best club for putting, no best grip, there is no best stance. Narrow to wide—square, open, closed—all are acceptable. (The rules, however, prohibit standing with either foot touching or astride the line of putt. The line extends from the hole to a point beyond the ball.)

Even though there is some variation in grip and stance among good players, there is a general consensus of opinion on basics to follow.

Basic Points for Addressing the Ball

- The club is held with a gentle firmness. The reverse-overlapping grip is favored.
- The club sole is flat on the ground with the clubface pointing to the target.
- The stance is taken close to the ball. The body is bent forward so that the eyes are directly above and looking straight down on the ball.
- The knees are bent and easy.
- The arms are relatively close to the body with the elbows bent. For steadiness the right arm may rest against the right thigh.
- Similar to all golf shots, the ball is played from a point opposite the inside of the left heel to a point opposite the center of the stance. If the ball is played toward the left side, more weight may be carried on the left foot.

Fig. 7.3. Putting stroke

THE SWING

The swing is a pendulum-like motion. The club is swung back and through close to the ground. For short distances the clubhead is swung on the intended line of ball roll. On long putts the feeling may be one of swinging the putterhead on the line, but as the swing increases in length the clubhead may naturally swing slightly inside the intended line of putt on the backswing and follow-through. Being overly concerned about the exact clubhead path tends to "freeze" the swing and create tension. Also, thinking about the path is distracting, for attention is then diverted from the real purpose of the swing—*to roll the ball into the hole.* Rather than trying to "harness" the stroke, let the swing develop naturally.

Having a feeling for the correct line of play and swinging the putter close to the ground should create this simple swing. The subtle combined movement of the hands, wrists, and arms will blend into one swing—one unit. In this pendulum-like swing the hands swing back and through with the clubhead. Avoid any detailed analysis of this swing; instead, work on developing a touch and feel for the stroke.

The body remains still. Its only contribution to the swing is to provide stability.

AIMING

To aim, simply draw an imaginary line of roll from the ball to the hole; then place the putter back of the ball so that the clubface is perpendicular to this line. On a straight putt, the clubface will point to the line and the hole; on a sidehill putt the clubface will point to a spot on the line, not to the hole. (On a sidehill putt, allowance must be made for the ball to roll down the sidehill.) The imaginary line of roll should be figured first from a position back of the ball, looking toward the cup. After the clubface is set so that it points to the target, the selected line of roll is confirmed. (Some players find it helpful to place the clubhead in front of the ball to check the alignment of the clubface.)

Make the procedure for addressing and stroking the ball simple. After setting the clubface so that it points to the target and taking a comfortable stance— sight down the intended line of roll, visualize the desired putt, then run your eyes back along the line to the ball. Proceed to putt without delay.

Your goal should be to roll the ball into the hole. If the ball does not roll into the cup, have it come to rest inches away, for an easy second putt. The adage "never up, never in" makes sense. *Putt the ball as far as the hole: only then does it have a chance to drop into the hole.*

JUDGMENT FACTORS

In addition to estimating distances, judgments must be made on how the ball will roll over the putting surface. "Reading the green" correctly is a must for good putting.

Putting greens are referred to as "fast" or "slow," depending upon how easily the ball will roll over the surface. If the grass is sparse, dried out, or newly mowed the green will be "fast." The opposite conditions will cause the green to be "slow." A bent type of grass influences the roll of the ball: a putt against the grain will require a firmer stroke than a putt rolling with the grain. Some allowance may have to be made when putting at an angle to the bent grass.

Figuring how the ball will roll over slopes and undulations (the "breaks" of the greens) is always interesting and many times rewarding. To aim five feet to one side of the hole, and then see your ball roll over your point of aim, gradually turn with the slope, and then drop into the hole, is indeed a joy.

Standing behind your ball while waiting your turn to putt gives you a chance to study the line and to figure any breaks. (see Rules of Etiquette) From this vantage point you can gather useful information by watching the roll of the putts made by other players.

PUTTING—THE KEY TO LOW SCORES

The top tournament professional golfers, men and women, often shoot sub-par rounds. The key stroke in their below-par rounds is putting. If a professional golfer were asked: "Of all the golf strokes, which one would you want at its peak during a tournament?" The answer would be unanimous: "Putting."

If par is 72 for a course, 36 strokes are allotted to reach the putting green and 36 strokes are assigned for putting. In a round of 18 holes, all players—from the novice to the professional—can often expect to take less than 36 putts, but rarely can players expect to take less than 36 strokes to reach the putting greens. Reaching a green in the par figure allotted for a hole is commonly called either "being on in regulation" or "hitting the green."

JIM BOOROS, Member, Advisory Staff, Acushnet Golf
Equipment

If you read that a professional "hit 18 greens" or was "on in regulation" on all 18 holes, you will know that the player was on the green in the distance allotment figures. What an opportunity for a fine score! On each hole this golfer is putting for a score of one under par, a birdie. If the player scores six birdies and twelve pars, taking a total of 30 putts, the score for a par-72 course will be a 66—a superb round of golf.

It would be most unusual for a player to take 36 putts and score below par for a round, because there are few greens, if any, that a player can reach in less than regulation figures. Par 5 holes for men and par 5 and par 6 holes for women can sometimes be reached in less than regulation by long hitters. If a player reaches the green of a par 5 hole in two shots or reaches the green of a par 6 hole in three shots, he or she is then putting for a score of 2 under par for the hole—an eagle. It is possible, but rare, for a player to reach the green of a par 4 hole in one stroke. The hole must be either especially short for its par or unusual conditions must exist, such as hard ground or wind aiding the distance of the shot from the tee.

Putting gives you chances to score under par on certain holes, as well as opportunities to make up for any error shots in your play from the tee to the putting green. *To score well, you must become a consistently good putter.*

PRACTICE SUGGESTIONS

- Use several golf balls and begin practice with the balls about a foot away from the hole. Simply stroke the balls into the cup with little or no thought on "how" to putt. Gradually increase the distance. Let your "instinct" for aiming and judging take over. If the ball does not fall into the cup, it should come to rest very close to the hole.
- Stroke the ball and listen for it to drop in the cup. This will help train you to remain calm and confident, not anxious about the result. The person who starts steering a putt immediately upon contacting the ball expects to miss the putt, not make it.
- Practice at home on carpeting. It does not matter if the surface is different from grass. You are practicing to develop a stroke and swing.
- When necessary, review some putting fundamentals. Then proceed to concentrate on sinking putts.
- After a session of starting with short putts and working back to long distances, try a variety of putts—short, long, uphill, downhill, sidehill, and from off the apron of the green. Practice lining up the putts without delay. Learn to size up the situation and proceed at once to make the putt.
- If in practice or play the putts are "rimming" the cup, with many close putts and "just misses," do not fret. You are putting well. The putts will start dropping so do not change this good stroke.
- On sidehill putts visualize the curved path on which the ball must roll to drop into the cup. Pick out a spot on this path for your point of aim—as a bowler might do in spot bowling. Use such points as a different colored section of grass or a dead blade of grass. (A dead blade of grass may be removed, but if it is an aid in aiming, make use of it. It will not deflect the roll of the ball.)

● Stroke the ball so that it will roll smoothly over the green. The ball should not bob up and down—it should "hug" the putting surface in a forward end-over-end roll—*overspin*. You can easily check the roll of the ball: draw a circumference line around the ball with a colored marking pencil, place the ball in a position so that the marked line is in the vertical plane, and then stroke the ball and check to see whether the line stays in the same plane.

● For self-testing practice, play nine different holes of a practice putting course. Par would be 18 for the nine holes. Check the number of strokes you are above or below par. Some of your practice may be in match or stroke competition with another player. This practice is enjoyable, stimulating, and challenging.

● After you have had some experience in putting, avoid analysis and details of action. Work on a smooth, easy, and comfortable stroke. Anyone who can swing a putter can learn to putt well. Good putting is up to you!

REVIEW QUESTIONS

1. A quiet, confident attitude is a necessity for good putting. How can a player develop confidence in putting?
2. Review some basic points for addressing the ball in putting. What stance is prohibited by the rules?
3. What are some useful suggestions to follow in practicing putting? How much analysis of the swing should be made?

special consideration shots
8

PLAYING FROM A BUNKER (Sand Trap)

To make golf more interesting and challenging, bunkers are placed strategically on the course. The rule book refers to these areas by the proper name, *bunkers;* many people, however, call them sand traps. In bunkers, creeks, and lakes (all defined as hazards), the surface of the area may not be touched before taking the forward swing to strike the ball. The club may not be grounded in the address position as in other shots. (It is permissible to take a practice swing, provided the surface of the hazard is not touched.)

Bunkers vary from course to course. Some are shallow, with a thin layer of sand spread over a hard surface; others, deep pits with almost vertical walls, and with soft powdery sand several inches thick. (A ball landing in some bunkers may bury itself.) The vision of standing in a pit with almost vertical walls and with the golf ball partially buried in the sand is dismal—yet, players of varying skills are able to hit outstanding shots in such circumstances.

The prime cue for all bunker shots is—hit the ball out of the bunker, do not be left with having to play another shot from the sand. Other useful tips for any sand play follow:

- Be willing to modify any distance objectives when playing from fairway traps. Use a club you feel sure about, one that will get the ball out of the bunker.
- To establish a stable stance, move your feet from side to side down into the sand. (Wiggle your feet into the sand.) A stance slightly wider than normal may also help provide stability.
- The rules prohibit testing the surface of the bunker. However, you cannot help but gather useful information about the condition of the sand and surface when you walk into the trap and when you take your stance.
- A shorter, more controlled swing may serve best in hitting distance shots from fairway bunkers. Such a swing may provide more accuracy so that the ball can be hit cleanly from the sand. A general recommendation for all sand shots is to limit body motion (pivot). (The less stable stance in sand warrants this consideration.)
- Always remember to swing the clubhead through the ball (or sand). Never try to "scoop" the ball. The hands must maintain a strong position through impact, especially in the "explosion shot."

From a shallow bunker with no overhanging turf (lip) and with the ball lying in a good position on the sand, few, if any, adjustments need to be made. From a fairway bunker use a club in which you have confidence. Aim to hit the ball before touching the sand with the clubhead. If the shallow trap is adjacent

Fig. 8.1. Addressing the ball—sand shot.

to the green, consider playing a stroke similar to a chip shot. Or, if after checking the area beyond the trap, you believe a ball can roll easily out of the sand and over the grass, then use the putter and putt the ball onto the green.

When the ball lies in a deep bunker bordered by overhanging turf, or when the ball is in a poor lie (partially buried or in a footprint) an "explosion shot" must be played. For this shot, use a sand wedge or the highest-lofted club in your set. Open the clubface when addressing the ball. Most players prefer taking an open stance. Whatever stance is taken, make it comfortable and plant your feet into the sand. Play the ball opposite the left side of the stance. Depending upon the sand texture and the desired distance, aim to strike the sand one to three inches back of the ball. Look at that selected spot, not at the ball. The clubhead sweeps through the sand and under the ball. Both the ball and the "cushion" of sand between the clubface and ball will be propelled forward at impact. It is important to complete the swing—to swing through the sand and the ball.

a.   b.

c.   d.

Fig. 8.2. MICHAEL HEMPHILL, "Explosion" shot from sand trap

PLAYING FROM HILLSIDES

In playing from hillside lies, follow the adage—"Don't make a mountain out of a molehill." In stroking the ball from a slight, gentle slope, play the shot almost as you would any comparable shot on level ground. Trust your instinctive sense of feel to guide you in taking a comfortable, balanced stance. When playing from steeper slopes, it may be necessary to make certain adjustments. Taking a practice swing on the slope is a valuable guide. You can get the feel for a balanced stance and for the automatic swing adjustments that will occur due to the different posture necessary in addressing the ball. Whatever your situation, keep your plans simple.

When playing from uphill or downhill lies, play the ball opposite an area favoring the higher side of the stance. An allowance in aiming should be made to counteract the tendency to hit the ball off line: when hitting uphill, aim slightly to the right; downhill, slightly to the left. (To avoid the possibility of accidentally moving the ball when addressing it; either place the clubhead farther back of the ball or hold it slightly above the ground.)

On sidehill lies with the ball above the feet, it may be helpful to take a shorter hold on the club (depending on the amount of slope). Keep your weight forward toward the toes to avoid falling back away from the ball on the swing.

Fig. 8.3. Uphill lie

Fig. 8.4. Downhill lie

Aim slightly right to compensate for the tendency to hit left. On a sidehill lie with the ball below the feet, settle your weight back toward the heels to avoid losing your balance forward, and aim slightly to the left.

PLAYING FROM THE ROUGH

Conditions in the rough vary. Sometimes there is little difference between the rough and the fairway, except that the turf off the fairway may be sparse. But when the grasses and undergrowth are long and heavy, and the ball nestles down into the area, problems arise. In such situations the only objective is to hit the ball out of the rough and onto a clear area.

To quickly send the ball into the air and above the rough, use a high-lofted club, and if necessary open the clubface. To avoid the interference of the long or heavy growth back of the ball, swing the clubhead more upright on the backswing. Maintain a firm, not tense, hold on the club throughout the stroke. Swing the clubhead through the ball and grass. (In addressing the ball or in removing loose impediments, be careful that you do not accidentally move the ball and incur a penalty of one stroke.)

PLAYING IN THE WIND

Playing golf in a strong wind is generally more difficult than playing on a calm day. "Don't fight the wind," is probably the best advice for play on windy days. Avoid "tensing up" and trying to do the impossible. Adapt your game to the conditions that exist, but do not completely abandon good scoring objectives.

Taking a shorter swing for distance shots may prove helpful—better balance can be maintained with the possibility of a more effective swing and more accurate shot results. Avoid speeding up your swing tempo to get distance.

When the wind is blowing the same direction as your intended long shots, take advantage of the situation—hit higher shots, letting the wind carry the ball farther. When the wind is blowing against you, hit low trajectory shots. If feasible, use a longer club for more distance, otherwise be satisfied with less than normal distance. If the wind is blowing across the line of play, aim your shot into the wind to allow for the carry of the ball in the wind direction.

To check the wind direction, note how the pennant on the flagstick is blowing, or toss some blades of grass into the air and note the direction and force of the wind.

REVIEW QUESTIONS

1. Review the important considerations a player should make in the following situations: ball is partially buried in a bunker adjacent to the putting green; ball is setting well up on the sand in a shallow bunker adjacent to the putting green; ball is lying in a heel print in a fairway bunker 180 yards from the hole.
2. What adjustments might you make in playing a ball from an uphill lie? From a downhill lie?

improving your golf game
9

ATTITUDE AND CONCENTRATION

- Confidence, the necessary ingredient for playing good golf, cannot be fantasy; it must be something real based on the experience of striking many successful golf shots. You, like thousands of other golfers, can develop and improve your skill in the game through practice and playing.
- Applying negative labels to yourself such as "I can't putt," "I can't aim," and "I can't use my 3-wood," leads to poor play. (Also, such statements spoken aloud are both boring and distracting to playing companions.)
- Accept the responsibilities for the shots you play. What someone else says or does should not affect your game adversely. Blaming anyone or any "bad break" for a poor shot makes little sense. Keep control of your game, then you can improve it.
- Golf requires patience and perseverance. Do not be disheartened by one or a few poor shots. An error shot may be a blessing in disguise—a fine recovery stroke may stimulate you to play an excellent round. Avoid letting yourself get "down"—you do not know what lies ahead, perhaps some brilliant shots.
- Golf requires concentration, exclusive attention to the shot being played, with no extraneous and disquieting thoughts. An often-heard expression about a poor shot is, "I didn't take enough time to concentrate." The implication that taking more time will assure concentration is erroneous. Time may allow disturbing and fearful ideas to enter into the planning. Be orderly and concise—select your objective, visualize the shot, and proceed to play the ball.
- "Playing" an opponent can take your mind off of your game. Let your worthy opponent be you—figure your best possible score for each hole and then compete against it. (fig. 9.1)
- Being too intent may take the joy out of golf and slow down your progress. Remember that a certain amount of relaxation is necessary to swing the club effectively, and remember golf is a game for pleasure. Enjoy it.

Fig. 9.1.

Chart Your Way To Better Golf

Charting your golf games can be enjoyable and interesting—and may help lower your scores.

Set a **Target Score** for each hole: the best, reasonable score you can make on the hole. Each time that pre-set score is made, encircle it on the score card. At the end of the round, total your 18-Hole Score and count the number of Target Scores.

Plot both scores on a chart similar to the sample graph. (The ranges you select for the 18-Hole Scores and the Target Scores may differ from those in the sample.) This player figured the range of Target Scores from 4 up to 14, and the 18-Hole Scores from 86 down to 76. (Note space was provided for even better scores.) The date, course, and course rating are recorded at the top of each score line.

Keeping these records may improve your game.

- Even if you score poorly on a hole early in a round, you will keep your enthusiasm and poise for playing well on the remaining holes. You will maintain your goal—to shoot a Target Score on each hole.
- Instead of "playing" an opponent, you will compete against your best scores, which is the best competition.

LESSONS

As long as you play golf you will take golf lessons—either from a golf teacher or from yourself in the form of self-coaching. This is the experience of all golfers, even the expert tournament professionals.

To profit most from lessons, follow reasonable practices.

- Work with your instructor. When you are taking lessons do not work on pet theories of your own. To do an effective job of teaching, your instructor must know what you are trying to do.
- When you are given a cue about your swing, do not expect a miracle to happen with the next shot. The result of a shot or two is not absolute proof of the worth or worthlessness of instruction.
- When a player tries to change a swing as per instruction, the change may feel drastic, yet little or no change may be visible to a teacher. At such times, the observation of the instructor should be trusted.
- In a golf class general instruction in the fundamentals and some individual coaching will be given. There is good reason for individual help—all swings do not develop the same. The coaching given one person may not be useful to another.
- Do not be disappointed and feel that you are failing to receive your "money's worth" if your instructor implies or says your swing looks fine and what you need is practice and play, not more instruction in swing analysis.

SELF-COACHING

Intelligent self-coaching builds your golf game; poor self-coaching destroys it. Your future golf game may be influenced most by your own teaching.

- If you find yourself with a persistent problem, you will probably save yourself much frustration and time if you take a lesson from a competent teacher instead of continuing to work alone.
- You can gather a mass of data on the golf swings—from reading, taking lessons, watching expert golfers in actions, and listening to other players. Be intelligent and discriminating in evaluating these ideas. Are the concepts sound and do they apply to you? Accumulating information has a bad and good side: you may "jam" your brain with too much data, or you may be enlightened by a new and different approach to the swing.
- When error shots "pop" into your game, do not panic and instantly begin a corrective program. Hitting a golf ball well requires precision. Anyone can have a lapse. If your stroke has been fairly consistent, give it a chance to return—do not tear it apart. If one club is giving you trouble, put it away and forget it. Later, practice with the club for short periods. Think about what to do right—NOT—"What did I do wrong?"
- Remember the hands are the connecting link with the club. They direct and transmit power. It is necessary to have a fine sense of control with the fingers and hands to stroke the ball well. Sense the hands directing and controlling clubhead action.

● Theories abound for hitting golf shots and correcting swings. At practice ranges you can get "free" lessons by asking almost any player for advice. The value of some pointers can be questioned. Many golfers like to tell their "secrets of success." Their advice varies from day to day: a tip that seems a miraculous cure one day is discarded the next day.

FITNESS FOR GOLF—SOME THOUGHTS

Many athletes participate in training programs to increase their skills and to avoid joint and muscle strain. Well-chosen exercises can help attain these goals as well as contribute to everyday good health. But what exercises should be chosen? Books, articles, and television programs overwhelm us with calisthenic choices—some good, some poor.

We seriously thought of including a series of conditioning exercises for golfers. After careful study we decided: first and most important, an exercise program should begin, not with exercise, but with the individual—a consideration of the person's needs, present capabilities, and physical habits. With this thought uppermost in our minds, we questioned presenting one series of exercises for all persons. Second, in the short space that we can allot to this subject in a golf book, we could not explore the necessary ramifications of exercise, such as precautions, uses, and exact details of performance. We concluded, therefore, that we could serve best by confining our writing to golf and to suggestions about how to make the best use of the physical activity of this game.

Perhaps the simplest and best advice for golfers is: if you now walk the course—*keep walking.* If at present you ride a motorized cart around the course, but are physically able to walk—*start walking.* If the course requires that you rent a shared cart, plan a way to do some walking. For instance, arrange with your riding partner to alternately ride and walk every other hole. If your clubs and bag are too heavy to carry on your shoulder, either use a hand cart or carry fewer clubs in a lightweight bag. (You may not even miss the clubs you decide not to carry.) Leg strength is essential in swinging a golf club effectively. Keep your leg muscles in good tone; and, treat your body and feet to the pleasure of treading on soft, grassy turf for about a three-mile distance. Walking is high on the list of good exercises for fitness.

A second prescription is: know what your body is capable of doing and know and accept its limitations. Use your body effectively—do not abuse it. Avoid attempting to swing a club in a fashion unsuitable to you.

The old cliché, "Keep your head down," leads overzealous followers of advice into trouble. On a full swing they attempt to keep their heads in the address position long after the ball has been struck. Besides destroying the swing through the ball, this attempted restriction can lead to a real pain in the neck!

A questionable swing cue for some players is to keep the left heel flat on the ground in the backswing of a full swing. Golfers with great flexibility may have no difficulty with this restriction. But for the less supple golfer, trying to coil the upper body while inhibiting the turn and natural "give" of the lower body and legs, is useless and risky. A free swing is difficult. Strenuously working one part of the back against a resisting part may cause a healthy back to become sensitive, and a sensitive one to become painful. (Most golfers allow the left heel to rise slightly from the ground in the backswing of a full swing.)

Nothing is so tempting to golfers as an idea to lengthen their drives. One cue for this universal wish is "get your body into the shot—shift your hips forward." Recalling the verse of a song may serve as a warning against taking this cue too seriously: "The thigh bone's connected to the hip bone, The hip bone's connected to the back bone, The back bone. . . ." With a "super distance" vision in mind, some golfers violently thrust their hips forward. But an exaggerated hip movement that does not blend in with the whole swing is useless, and it may render a person unfit for golf (suffering from a sacro-iliac sprain and painful distress signals).

Golf swings vary because people vary. Fortunately, we can all develop form that suits our particular body-build and condition. When golfers attempt to move (or restrict movement) in ways that tax the body's natural ability, nothing is gained and a good deal may be lost.

Practice away from the course and practice range (A Home Practice Plan) can pay off with no cost to you. A small amount of relaxation time, a golf break, can help improve your strokes and help you stay in condition for golf. Through practice swinging and exercises you can train yourself to move in good form. You can deposit correct movements in your "muscle memory bank."

Here is a starting program. Make adaptations as you see fit, but keep the plan simple—complicated exercise programs are often quickly abandoned and forgotten. Gradually increase the time you swing and do the exercises. Use your good judgment on what is a worthwhile program for you. (see also Ch. 4–7 Practice Suggestions. Also, remember, before you swing a club be certain no one is within range of your swing. Check your practice area before you swing a club.)

- Practice the putting swing without stroking a ball. Practice putting a ball to a target.
- Practice the one-quarter, one-half, three-quarter, and full swings without hitting balls.
- Practice handling the club—make it a familiar tool. Draw "air figures" with the clubhead, such as figure 8's and circles. (fig. 9.2a)
- Point the clubhead forward and back over your right shoulder. Note the responsive wrist action. (fig. 9.2b)
- Swing (with or without a club) as if you were swinging a baseball bat. Start swinging to hit a ball at shoulder height, then waist height, and then an imaginary ball on the ground. Let the body and legs respond to the movement. Keep the swing easy and smooth—do not try to hit home runs. (fig. 9.3)
- Practice the exercises for foot, leg, and body action. Stay relaxed. (fig. 9.4)

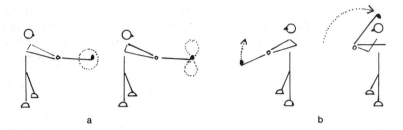

Fig. 9.2. *a,* Drawing air figures; *b* Pointing clubhead

Fig. 9.3. Baseball swing with and without club

Fig. 9.4. Foot, leg, and body exercises

EXAMINATION OF SOME ERROR SHOTS

Topping

A topped ball is hit above its center, thus imparting topspin to the ball. (fig. 9.5) The ball may travel in the air a short distance and then dive to the ground, or it may just roll along the ground.

Attempting to "hit the ball up into the air" or "get under the ball" often results in a topped shot. With such incorrect ideas in mind, the player is apt to swing the clubhead sharply upward through the impact zone, thus contacting the ball above its center. The strong, upward clubhead action causes the head and body to move up. The body weight may fail to shift properly to the left foot; in extreme cases the weight may shift back to the right side with the left heel coming off the ground.

Another common error causing a topped shot is changing the focus of attention from the execution of the stroke to its result. Instead of completing a good swing through the ball, the tense and anxious player looks up quickly to see, "What happened!?"

The early upward motion of the head at ball contact has fostered the most widely used correction of golf swings: "Keep your head down." The problem with using only this cue is that the real error is not addressed. The ball is topped with the clubhead—not the cranium head. To correct the error of topping, attention should be centered on the cause of the error, incorrect clubface and ball contact—not on one symptom.

The following cues can be helpful in eliminating the error of topping:

● Select the correct purpose for the swing: to contact the ball squarely and hit it to the target. The clubface loft, not any swing effort, will loft the ball into the air.
● Focus your attention on the complete swing. Be patient about seeing the shot result.
● Avoid flinching through the impact area. The act of drawing away from the ball with the shoulders and arms pulls the clubhead up. Keep the shoulders and arms "easy."

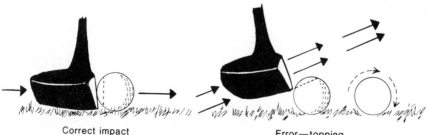

Correct impact   Error—topping

Fig. 9.5.

- Swing the clubhead low through the impact area. If the ball is hit from a tee, sweep out the tee as the ball is struck; if from the grass, sweep the grass after striking the ball.
- In addressing the ball, instead of looking at the top of the ball, watch a spot at the back of the ball where contact should be made.
- Think: "Hit the ball so it will travel low." With this thought in mind, the clubhead is likely to be swung close to the ground through impact.

Striking the Ground Before Ball Contact—"Fat" Shot

This error may be related to topping if an attempt is made to "scoop" the ball into the air. Quick, violent exertions in the impact area can also result in "fat" shots. To correct the error, discard any purpose of trying to "scoop" the ball into the air. Once a player hits several "fat" shots, especially short pitch shots, a feeling of apprehension arises when another such shot must be played. Such fears can be dispelled and the error corrected by practice on the practice range. (see Ch. 5: Grip, Hand Action, and Wrist Action; also fig. 9.6)

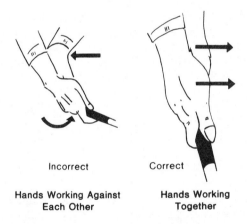

Incorrect

Correct

**Hands Working Against
Each Other**

**Hands Working
Together**

Fig. 9.6. Hand action through impact

Shanking the Ball

If shanking the ball were a common fault, the population of golfers might decrease considerably. Shanking may be the most exasperating error in golf. This shot is hit with an iron and the ball is contacted near the neck of the club, the rounded surface at the heel of the clubface. When the ball is struck with this rounded surface, the ball "squirts" out to the right. The feeling the player experiences is horrendous, one of total ineffectiveness. There are fortunate golfers who have never or rarely shanked a shot. Those unfortunate players who go through periods of shanking might do better seeing a psychiatrist than seeing a golf teacher. The word "shank" is taboo in golf conversation—golfers fear that the mere mention of the word will bring on the error! Opinions on corrections

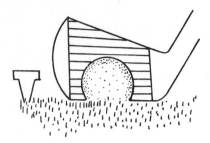

Fig. 9.7. Avoiding a shank.

vary and volumes could be written on the subject. The following are possible corrections:

● Go back to the simple, practice hitting short approach shots with a medium iron and work up to longer iron shots. Unless the swing is completely off, this may be the best correction—working on the positive and not fighting a fault.
● Picking up the club on the backswing and applying extra effort either at the start of the downswing or near ball impact can force the clubhead forward and outside of the intended ball flight line. Placing a tee in the ground just beyond the ball and then swinging to avoid hitting the tee can help keep the clubhead in the correct path.
● Check the spot on the clubface where the ball is addressed. Addressing the ball out toward the toe of the clubface to allow for any error may be of temporary help.

EXAMINATION OF DIRECTIONAL FLIGHT ERRORS

Why a golf shot travels off line to the right or left of the intended target should not be a mystery. To demonstrate how you can stroke a ball off line try this experiment using a putter. Putt a ball to a target about five feet away. Then keeping the same stance and grip, putt a ball to the right of the target. Now stroke a ball so that it will roll to the left of the original target. If the ball rolled straight to the right or left, the putter face was at right angles to the clubhead path. If the ball rolled with clockwise or counter-clockwise spin, then the clubface was not perpendicular to the path of the club.

In baseball or softball, players hit balls to left, center, and right fields by timing the swings so that the bat faces the target at impact. No change of stance is necessary. In tennis or table tennis, players have no difficulty in hitting shots to right, center, or left courts; they even purposely put spin on the ball to deceive their opponents.

Whether the sports implement to strike a ball is a golf club, bat, or racket, the position of the striking surface and its path at ball contact determine the flight of the ball. This is basic information to use when examining errors in the directional flight of the golf ball.

Push and Slice

Both shots travel to the right of the intended target. In a push *shot* the path of the clubhead through the contact area is on a line toward the right of the target and the clubface is perpendicular to this line. This produces a straight shot but off line to the right. In a *slice,* the path of the clubhead through contact can vary, but the clubface in relation to the path is open or facing to the right. This contact produces a horizontal, clockwise spin on the ball. As the spinning ball travels through the air, the ball will curve to the right.

In considering corrections for these errors, assume that the grip and stance are correct and that the swing appears to be in good form.

- Being a fraction late in swinging the clubface to the square position at ball contact will result in error shots to the right. The ever-present urge to add effort at impact may cause the player to push the handle, leaving the clubface open. Also, a "quitting action" caused by anxiety and fear prevents the face from reaching the square position. Instead of confidently swinging the clubhead and maintaining the correct swing posture through impact, the player rises up ("comes off the ball") and leaves the clubface pointing to the right. Directing attention to swinging the clubface to the square position should help correct these errors.
- If leaving the clubface open at impact has been a persistent problem, it may feel as if the clubface is closed when it is finally swung to the square position. (But the proof here is not in the feel—it is in the flight of the ball.) In some cases where the wrong feeling has been established, it is necessary to exaggerate—to try to swing the clubface to the closed position at ball contact. If after such an attempt, the ball travels straight to the target, the face was square at impact—no matter what the player felt. If the ball travelled to the left, an overcorrection was made.

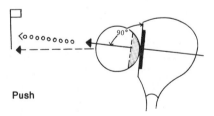

Push

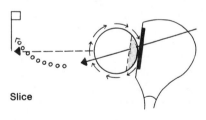

Slice

Push—Straight shot to right of target
- Clubhead path through impact is on a line toward the right of the target—from inside-out.
- Club face is perpendicular to the clubhead path.

Slice—Ball curves to right due to clockwise (horizontal) spin
- Clubhead path through impact can be: (1) On a line to the target, (2) From outside-in, (3) From inside-out.
- Club face is pointing to the right of the clubhead path.

Fig. 9.8. Push and slice

- When the ball first travels to the left and then curves to the right of the intended target, the clubhead path is from "outside-in." This action may be the result of trying to avoid a slice, trying to steer the ball away from the right. The cure may be taking many practice swings in the correct path. Visualize the correct path through impact and swing on that line. Cut a swath of grass with the clubhead to check the path.
- Avoid trying to steer the ball straight or to get a straight follow-through. Trust that the swiftly swinging clubhead will travel in the correct path and strike the ball squarely.
- A poor correction is aiming to the left of the target. Such a practice fails to correct the error and usually compounds it.

An often-heard correction for slicing is "hit from inside out." This may have some value for the person who has a very distorted swing, with the clubhead travelling from far outside and across the intended line of flight. Following only the cue, "swing from inside out," may increase the error of hitting to the right. The path of the clubhead through the contact area should be from inside the intended line—on the intended line—and then inside again.

A closed stance is suggested frequently to correct slicing. If the player takes a closed stance and has a feeling of aiming to the right, and then compensates for this aim by swinging the clubface over to direct the ball to the intended target, this stance would be an aid. But changing the stance does not necessarily change the direction of the shot—trick shot artists prove this. They can take any stance, stand on one foot, or even sit down and hit the ball any direction they choose. The path of the clubhead through the impact area and the relation of the clubface to this path determines the directional flight of the ball.

Pull and Hook

Both shots travel to the left of the intended target. In the *pull shot* the path of the clubhead through the contact area is on a line toward the left of the target and the clubface is perpendicular to this line. This produces a straight shot but off line to the left. In a *hook shot* the path of the clubhead can vary, but the clubface in relation to the clubhead path is closed or facing to the left. This contact produces a horizontal counter-clockwise spin of the ball. As the spinning ball travels through the air, the ball will curve to the left (fig. 9.9). The errors of pulling and hooking are less common than those of pushing and slicing. Consider the following in correcting the pull or hook.

- Check the grip, especially the right hand. If the club is held with the right palm facing skyward, an error shot to the left is likely to occur. During the swing the right hand is apt to return to a more natural position, thus closing the clubface.
- To change a habit of swinging the clubhead to a closed position at impact, it may be necessary to try to swing the clubhead through the ball with a feeling that the clubface is open. If the ball travels straight after such an effort, the clubface was square at ball contact.
- Trying to hit the ball an extra long distance and "slapping" at the ball often results in hooking the ball. The right hand overpowers the left in the impact

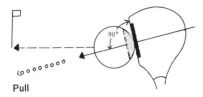

Pull

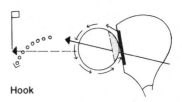

Hook

Pull—Straight shot to left of target
- Clubhead path through impact is on a line toward the left of the target—from outside-in.
- Club face is perpendicular to clubhead path.

Hook—Ball curves to left due to counterclockwise (horizontal) spin
- Clubhead path through impact can be: (1) On a line to the target, (2) From inside-out, (3) From outside-in.
- Club face is pointing to the left of the clubhead path.

Fig. 9.9. Pull and hook

zone, thus closing the clubface. When this error is corrected the player may sense a dramatic change in the swing. It may feel as though the left hand and arm are in control of the downswing and follow-through, and that the right hand is doing little or nothing to strike the ball.

● If there is a consistent error of pulling the ball to the left of the target, check the stance and the ball position in relation to the feet. When a player pulls a ball it may be obvious that he or she has turned the body too early in the impact zone. Fear of hitting to the right may cause a player to turn on the ball to direct the ball away from such an error shot.

At times skilled players will intentionally strike a ball so that it curves in flight and ends up on target. The *draw* shot curves in flight from right to left; the *fade* shot, from left to right.

PLAYING HINTS

● Be ready to play golf. Warm up before you play. Before stepping on the first tee, practice swinging the club, starting with the short swing; do the exercises for handling the club and for the body motion. (fig. 9.2, 9.3, 9.4) Do gentle stretching exercises and hold the stretch a few seconds. (Avoid violent or "bouncing" exercises.) Make easy movements which will relax the area through the shoulders and neck. As you play your round stay "easy" so that you can use your muscles efficiently.
● Learn the golf rules. Ignorance of the rules may cost you penalty strokes. Privileges extended by the rules may prove advantageous; for instance, when you drop a ball back of a water hazard, you may choose a well-kept area of grass on which to drop the ball, provided all the other provisions of the rules are followed.
● Play according to the rules and keep your score accurately. To do otherwise is deceiving yourself.
● Golf should be a congenial and friendly game. When all players are considerate of each other, the game is enjoyable. The golf course is not the place for a lot of talk and idle chatter.

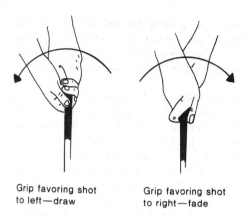

Grip favoring shot
to left—draw

Grip favoring shot
to right—fade

Fig. 9.10.

- If the course is in poor condition, improving the lie of the ball on the fairway ("preferred lies" or "winter rules") may be condoned. Continued play of "winter rules," however, is not golf. Accept the game's challenge—play the ball as it lies.
- Do not complain about the course. You choose the course; it does not choose you.
- No instruction on how to swing a club should be given during a round. Swing cues given during play are seldom appreciated; usually, they are distracting to both "coach" and "student."
- Assume you are teeing off at a hole with an out of bounds along the right side of the fairway. Tee the ball toward the right side of the teeing area, and aim to shoot to the center or slightly left of center of the fairway. In similar circumstances, use this strategy of aiming away from trouble.
- Tee up the ball when shooting an iron shot from the tee. It is easier to hit a ball from a tee than from the ground. To avoid possible interference by the tee when hitting with a high-lofted iron (the tee and the ball could be contacted simultaneously), loosen the turf (especially hard ground) around the tee as you place it in the turf, or use a broken tee. If the tee is struck, it can fly out of the ground easily, offering no resistance. (fig. 9.11)

Fig. 9.11.

- Think of and play one shot at a time. Have a clear purpose for each stroke. Avoid building up concern and tension about the next shot. For example, you see your ball roll into a distant bunker. There is no way to play the ball until you reach the trap—relax. When you get to the bunker, size up the situation, plan the shot, and play it.
- To select the correct club for a shot, consider: (1) the lie of the ball, (2) the desired distance, (3) special requirements for the situation, (4) course conditions, and (5) your skill with the different clubs. If the choice is between two clubs in which you have equal confidence, play the longer club to the green. Being short of the green, "underclubbing," is a common fault of golfers.
- Learn different distances to the green by spotting various objects such as trees, bushes, and bunkers. Learn the "breaks" of the greens. Plan the most advantageous way to play each hole. Adjust your game to the course.
- If the ball is lying in a difficult position, on sparse grass or on bare ground, take a practice swing over a spot similar in nature (if such a spot is near your ball). You have then faced the situation and will be less apt to be concerned about the lie.
- Play a safe shot if a daring one might put you in great trouble. If playing a safe shot costs an extra stroke to reach the green, a one-putt green may make up for the stroke.
- Play your own game of golf. If your distance limit for a 7-iron is 120 yards, do not be challenged to hit a 7-iron 140 yards because a member of your group can do so. Your objective is to score well, not to compete in a distance contest.
- Keep a record of your putts. In a corner of the scoring square for each hole, place a number indicating putts for the hole.
- Study your game after playing. If the game was fair or poor, what caused the trouble? Your swing? Carelessness? Lack of concentration? No warm-up? Too many putts? What are the solutions? If, however, you played a good or superb game, relax and enjoy the good feeling. You may even sit back and contemplate: "If a couple more of those putts had dropped. . . ."

INSTRUCTIONS FOR THE NEW PLAYER

Your first experiences in playing golf can be especially pleasant if you are prepared to go on the course—if you have acquired some skill in the strokes and have a good general knowledge of the game.
- You should be able to answer "YES" to these questions:
  —Are you able to sink many putts of two to three feet in length?
  —On longer putts of 25 feet or more, can you hole out in two strokes 50% of the time?
  —Have you developed some consistency in hitting shorter approach shots? Do you know which clubs to use for chip and pitch shots? Do you know how much to "choke up" on the club and how much swing to take for various distances, such as 20, 40, and 60 yards?

—Have you developed some consistency in hitting the ball with the full swing? Do you know approximately how far you can hit the ball with each of the clubs in your set?

—Have you carefully studied and learned the safety precautions, the etiquette, and the golf rules? Are you willing to watch the conduct of the experienced golfer and to learn from your observations?

● These suggestions will help you:

—If available, play a course consisting of short holes. If your only choice is a full length course, plan your game when the course is not crowded.

—If possible, have an experienced golfer guide you in correct conduct. But remember, no lengthy or detailed instruction should be asked for or given while playing on the course.

—You will most likely take more strokes than other players. You can help make up the time by walking rapidly between shots and by being alert to play in your group. Avoid delaying play.

—If necessary, be willing to modify your game so you will not delay the play of others. For example, you have made several attempts to hit the ball from deep rough without success. Either pick up your ball and toss it in the fairway; or, discontinue play on the hole and resume play at the next tee. You will be relieved of concern and tension; your playing companions and other golfers on the course will appreciate your thoughtful consideration. Scores for early games are not so important that they merit delaying play.

—Golf is a complicated game. Be patient. With practice, study, and experience you will soon be playing golf as it should be played.

REVIEW QUESTIONS

1. How does the ball flight differ in the slice and push shots? Describe how the clubface must contact the ball to produce these shots. What are some possible corrections for these errors?

2. Why may trying to hit the ball up into the air cause the very error it is intended to correct? What are some possible corrections for the error of topping the ball?

3. Slow play continues to be a problem on the golf course. How can you, no matter what your skill, help alleviate this problem?

4. What steps can you take to improve your game and enjoy it more?

essential knowledge
10

No matter what your golfing skill, in golf knowledge and procedures you can be well-informed. You can make yourself a welcome member of any golfing group by knowing and observing the accepted traditional conventions of the game.

ETIQUETTE

The rules of etiquette are not strict formalities that complicate play; rather, they simplify and enhance the game. Observance of these rules makes it possible to play better golf and enjoy the game more, to keep the course in good condition, and to allow more people to play golf by speeding up play. Strict adherence to the rules of etiquette should be routine practice for all players.

Creating a Quiet Atmosphere

1. You and all golfers have a common purpose—to play your best game. Considerate and courteous actions set the stage for accomplishing this goal.
2. Good golf requires concentration. Remain quiet when a player is either preparing to play or playing a shot.
3. Stand quietly and out of range of any player making a stroke. Stand out of any line of play. (The line of play extends from in back of the ball, through the ball, and beyond the target.)
4. Be careful not to disturb players outside your group. For example, the noise of loud talk will carry to other parts of the course, thus distracting players in other areas.
5. Frustrations resulting from hitting unsatisfactory shots or getting "bad breaks" are not justifications for unpleasant behavior. Complaining, using offensive language, and club throwing are examples of unacceptable actions.

Care of the Golf Course

1. Replace all divots and press them firmly in place. Avoid taking divots with practice swings.

2. Walk carefully on the putting green to avoid marring the surface. Do not step or stand at the edge of the hole (cup). (On the practice putting green, stand away from any hole when playing the ball to another cup.)
3. Repair ball marks on the green. Either with a tee or with a fork-like metal tool (available at golf shops for a nominal cost) lift up and press back the grass around the pit mark, leaving a level surface.
4. After removing the flagstick from the hole, lay it down—do not drop or throw it on the green.
5. After putting out, lift the ball out of the cup with your hand. Do not twist the putter blade within the cup to retrieve the ball. Such a practice can mar the walls and edges of the cup.
6. Keep all carts (motorized and hand) well away from the greens and aprons, and off the teeing areas. When driving motorized carts, stay on the cart paths as much as possible.
7. When leaving a bunker, smooth out the surface so that its condition is as good or better than when you entered it.
8. Do not discard litter on the course. Do your part in maintaining the beauty of the golf course.

Playing without Delay

1. Remember, you are one of many golfers paying for the privilege of playing on the course. Do your part—play without delay—follow practices that will help speed up play.
2. If you are new to the game, be ready to play. Have a knowledge of safety, etiquette, and rules and possess basic skills in the strokes before you attempt to play on the course. (See Ch. 9, Instructions for the New Player)
3. You will need your own set of clubs, golf bag, balls, and tees. During play do not borrow clubs from another player.
4. Before starting a round, note the name and number of your golf ball. To easily identify your ball, follow the USGA recommendation—place a distinguishing mark on the ball. When your ball is in play, as on the fairway, do not pick up the ball to identify it; instead, look around it and note the make, number, and any identification mark.
5. Avoid delaying play by taking numerous practice swings. (If any practice swings are taken, try to limit the number to one or two.)
6. Be ready to play when it is your turn. It is possible to plan ahead for some strokes. (see Ch. 7 Putting)
7. Any instruction should be incidental, if at all. There should not be any delay because one person is attempting to teach another.
8. After you hit a shot, watch the ball and "spot" its position carefully, so you can walk directly to it. Also, watch the stroke results of other players in your group so that you can help in any search for a ball.
9. When your ball is on the wrong fairway, permit players playing that hole to have the right-of-way. Avoid interfering with other players. (Before entering another fairway, be sure it is safe to do so.)
10. If your group is delaying play by failing to keep its place (falling behind the group ahead by one clear hole) either speed up your play and regain your

proper position or invite the following group to pass. If you invite the following group to play through, wait until they are out of range before resuming play. (If you are extended the courtesy of playing through, express your appreciation.)

11. At some golf courses on par-3 holes, it is a practice for golfers who have reached the putting green to invite players of the following group to hit their tee shots. While waiting for the group behind to shoot, the players on the green should stand behind the green, off the putting surface, and to one side of the line from the tee to the flagstick.

On the Putting Green

1. Place your golf bag or cart well off and to one side or back of the green nearest the next tee.
2. Do not step or stand in any line of play. Check your shadow—see that it does not cast in another player's line of putt or over the hole.
3. Mark and lift your ball when requested to do so. To mark your ball's position, place a small coin or marker behind the ball and then lift the ball. If your ball is in the line of another player's putt, after placing the coin behind the ball, measure out the necessary putterhead lengths to one side, and move the coin to this spot. In stroke play the player may either mark or play the ball. The option of playing the ball usually speeds up play. Never choose to hole out if you would have to stand in someone's line of putt.
4. When attending the flagstick, stand to one side of the cup, at arm's length, and hold the stick and the flag (if within reach). See that your shadow does not cast in the line of play. The stick should be held in the center of the cup until removal is necessary. After removing the pin, lay it down where it will not interfere with play. When all players are on the putting green or close to it, a player whose ball lies close to the hole usually offers to attend the flagstick.
5. After your group has holed out, replace the flagstick, leave the green immediately, and proceed to the next tee. Never remain on the green to review play of the hole or to mark scores on the score card. Do not take practice shots that will delay play.

In the Bunker

1. Leave your golf bag or cart well outside the edge of the bunker.
2. Enter the bunker at the lowest bank and take the shortest route to the ball.
3. Before you walk into a bunker to play your shot, check to see whether the rake is nearby. If it is not, secure and place it near you, but where it will not interfere with play. With the rake close at hand, you can rake the sand as you walk from the trap.
4. Never enter or stand in a bunker when another golfer is playing from it.
5. On leaving the sand trap, rake or in some manner smooth out all footprints and marks, thus leaving the surface of the sand in perfect condition.

RULES

This summary of selected rules is an introduction to your study of the complete rules. It is only a digest and is not a substitute for the official rules as published by the United States Golf Association. (Copies of the rules are available at local golf shops or from the USGA, Far Hills, NJ 07931.)

All golfers should have a thorough knowledge of the rules—only then can they play golf properly. It is recommended that all players carry an up-to-date rule book in their golf bags.

Types of Competition

The two main types of golf competition are *stroke play* and *match play*. In stroke play the person with the lowest score for the stipulated number of rounds, usually four rounds (72 holes) is the winner. If two or more players are tied for first place at the end of a tournament, these players either play an 18-hole round; or they play one or more extra holes and the first player to make the low score on a hole is the winner. (The committee in charge determines the method of playing off ties in tournaments.) In stroke competition, all players are properly referred to as *competitors,* except within a playing group the contestants are called *fellow-competitors.*

Match play competition is based on scores for each hole, not total score for a round. In a single match a player competes against only one other player, the *opponent.* They play until one person is more holes ahead than there are holes remaining to be played in the match. If the match is tied at the end of the stipulated round, usually players continue play until one player wins a hole. Match play is an elimination type tournament, so in the final round there are only two players remaining to compete for the championship.

Match Play Score Card

Assume that at the end of nine holes, Bill is 1 hole up on Joe. Hole #10 is tied or halved. Bill remains 1 up. Joe wins #11. The match is all square. Joe wins #12 and #13. Joe is 2 up. Hole #14 is halved. Joe wins #15 and is now 3 up with 3 holes remaining to be played. Joe is dormie 3. (A player is dormie when he is the same number of holes up as there are holes remaining to be played.) Hole #16 is halved. Joe wins the match, 3 holes up with 2 remaining, or simply 3 and 2 (3–2).

HOLE NO.	10	11	12	13	14	15	16	17	18
Bill (1 up)	5	5	4	7	4	4	4	—	
	o	–	–	–	o	–	o		
Joe (1 down)	5	3	3	5	4	3	4	—	
	o	+	+	+	o	+	o		

Fig. 10.1. Match play card

Rules for Teeing Off

1. Play is started at each hole by teeing the ball within the limits of the teeing area. This area is bounded in front by two tee markers and extends two club lengths back of the markers.
2. Honor, the privilege of teeing first, is usually decided by lot on the first tee. After the first hole, the honor is decided by scores on the previous hole. The person with the lowest score shoots first and the others follow according to their scores. If two or more players score the same on a hole, they tee off in the order they followed on the previous tee.
3. A ball is not in play until a stroke is made from the tee. If a player in addressing the ball, not yet in play, accidentally knocks the ball off the tee, it may be teed again without penalty.

General Rules

1. After teeing off, players continue to strike the ball, in turn, until they hole out. The ball should be played as it lies and not be touched except to strike it, unless situations or rules require or permit otherwise.
2. The ball farthest from the hole is played first. (Except stroke play, a player may putt out instead of marking a ball.)
3. Any attempt to hit the ball is counted as a stroke, whether or not the ball is struck.
4. If after addressing the ball in play, the ball moves, the penalty is one stroke and the ball must be played as it lies.
5. Through the green, if after moving a loose impediment within one club-length of the ball, the ball moves before the player has addressed it, the penalty is one stroke and the ball must be replaced. If a player moves an obstruction and the ball moves, the ball is replaced without penalty. When a player accidentally moves a ball when searching for it in areas such as casual water, ground under repair, or a hole or runway made by a burrowing animal, the ball is replaced without penalty.
6. When the ball is in play, the player may not press or stamp down ground, or break, bend, or remove anything fixed or growing.
7. Loose impediments such as fallen leaves, pebbles, worms, and insects that interfere with play may be moved. Except, if the ball lies in a hazard, loose impediments may not be moved.
8. Movable obstructions such as water hoses, trash containers, and benches that interfere with play may be moved.
9. In certain situations, a player may lift or be required to lift a ball and drop or place it. To drop a ball, a player stands erect, facing any direction; holds the ball at shoulder height with the arm extended; and drops the ball. The ball must not come to rest nearer the hole than its original position. (In the continuing summary, when the words, "the player drops the ball," are used, assume that the ball is dropped properly and not nearer the hole.)
10. When a ball lies on a wrong putting green, the ball must be lifted and dropped off the green within one club-length of the nearest point of relief without penalty.

11. Obstructions such as paved cart paths, shelters, and sprinkler heads are immovable obstructions. (It is important to note that walls, fences, stakes, and railings defining out of bounds are not obstructions. No relief is allowed without penalty.) If a ball lies in or on an immovable obstruction, or if the obstruction interferes with the player's stance or swing through the green, the ball may be lifted and dropped within one club-length of the nearest point of relief without penalty. In the bunker, the ball must be dropped within the bunker. If on the putting green, the already stated conditions exist, or if the obstruction is situated between the ball on the green and the hole, the ball may be lifted and *placed* at the nearest point of relief without penalty. In a water hazard, no relief is allowed without penalty.

12a. If a ball lies in casual water or when casual water interferes with a player's stance or swing through the green, the ball may be lifted and dropped within one club-length of the nearest point of relief without penalty. If this condition exists in a bunker, the ball may be either dropped in the bunker without penalty, or dropped ouside the bunker with a penalty of one stroke. (see line of drop under Water Hazard Rule) If on the putting green the already stated conditions exist, or if the area of casual water is between the ball on the green and the hole, the ball may be lifted and *placed* at the nearest point of relief, without penalty.

12b. The rule for relief from casual water applies to other situations, such as ground under repair, and a hole, runway, or cast made by a burrowing animal. Except when the ball lies in a water hazard, no relief is allowed from a hole, runway, or cast from a burrowing animal.

13. You may ask only your caddie, partner, or partner's caddie for advice regarding the play of a stroke.

14. If another player's ball interferes with your play, you may request the ball be marked and lifted.

15. The general penalty for breaking a rule in stroke play is two strokes; in match play, loss of hole. For example, a player removes leaves from a sand trap, or stamps down the grass in back of the ball lying on the fairway— the penalty is two strokes in stroke play and loss of hole in match play.

16. The score card should be checked for local rules and interpretations which apply to the course being played.

Rules for the Putting Green (See Ch. 7—Stance for Putting)

1. When playing the ball from the putting green, request that the flagstick be attended or removed from the hole. The penalty for playing a ball from the green and having it strike the flagstick is two strokes in stroke play and loss of hole in match play.

2. In stroke play, if a ball played from the putting green strikes a fellow-competitor's ball (also on the green) the penalty is two strokes. If the fellow-competitor's ball is moved by the impact, it must be replaced.

3. In match play there is no penalty for a player's ball played from the putting green striking the opponent's ball, also on the green. If the opponent's ball is moved by the impact, it must be replaced.

4. Sand and loose soil are loose impediments on the putting green only. They may be picked up or brushed aside with the hand or club. If the ball is accidentally moved in removing loose impediments on the green, it is replaced without penalty.
5. When any part of the ball overhangs the hole, the player, after walking to the hole without delay, may wait ten seconds. If the ball does not fall into the hole in that time, it is considered to be at rest.

Rules for Hazards

1. By USGA definition there are two types of hazards: bunkers and water hazards (including lateral water hazards). A bunker is usually a depressed area of bare ground covered with sand, frequently called a sand trap. Grass-covered areas within or surrounding the bunker are not parts of the hazard. The grass-covered area or any dry ground within the indicated margins of the water hazard are part of the hazard. The limits of water hazards are usually defined by stakes or lines.
2. When the ball lies in a hazard, loose impediments may not be moved.
3. Man-made objects, such as a rake, may be moved.
4. In addressing the ball in a hazard, the club may not be grounded. The surface of the hazard cannot be touched before taking the forward swing to strike the ball.
5a. If a ball is lost in a water hazard or impossible to play, the player may proceed under the following options:
   A. Drop a ball under penalty of one stroke at the spot from which the original ball was played. If the original ball was played from the tee, the ball may be teed anywhere in the teeing area.
   B. Drop a ball under penalty of one stroke any distance behind the hazard, keeping the spot at which the ball last crossed the margin of the hazard between the player and the hole.

In situation A, Figure 10.2, it is to the player's advantage to shoot stroke 3 from the tee. In situation B, too much yardage would be lost by playing the ball from the tee. Therefore, a player would usually drop a ball any distance back of the hazard on the drop line indicated and shoot stroke 3.

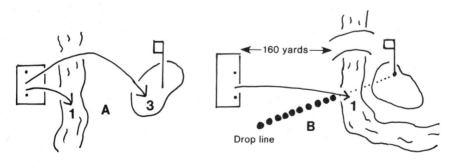

Fig. 10.2. Water hazard

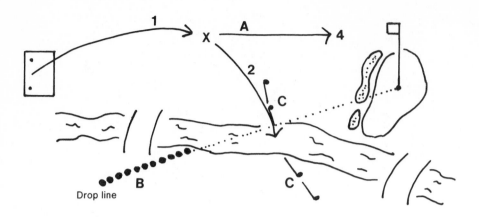

Fig. 10.3. Lateral water hazard

5b. For a lateral water hazard, a player may either play in accordance with A or B in item 5a, or:
C. Under penalty of one stroke, the ball may be dropped within two club-lengths of where the ball last crossed the margin of the hazard; or within two club-lengths of a point an equal distance from the hole on the opposite margin of the hazard, but not nearer the hole. (see fig. 10.3) Option A, drop ball at X. Option B, drop ball on indicated drop line. Option C, drop ball within two club-lengths of either side of the hazard.

Ball Out of bounds, Lost Ball, Provisional Ball

1. A ball is out of bounds when it lies on ground on which play is disallowed. The area is usually marked by a fence or out-of-bounds stakes.
2. A player is allowed five minutes to search for a ball. After that time the ball is considered lost.
3. If a ball is out of bounds or is lost outside of a water hazard, the penalty is loss of distance and one stroke. The player shoots again from where the original ball was played and adds one penalty stroke. (Figure 10.4)
4. When a ball is hit that may be out of bounds or may be lost outside of a water hazard, a provisional ball may be played. For example, you hit a long drive from the tee toward an out-of-bounds fence. From the distant view, you cannot be sure whether the ball is in or out of bounds. After informing your playing companions of your intention, you may hit another ball, a provisional ball. If the original ball is in bounds, play it and pick up the provisional ball. If the original ball is out of bounds, play the provisional ball. (Stroke and distance penalty applies.) Playing a provisional ball for one that may be out of bounds or lost (outside of a water hazard) saves the time and trouble of going back to the original spot of play to hit another ball.

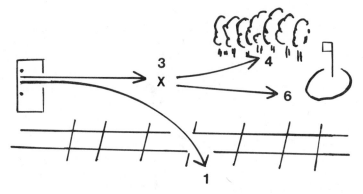

Fig. 10.4. Stroke and distance penalty—out of bounds and lost ball

Stroke and Distance Penalty

A player drives out of bounds (1). He tees another ball, adds a penalty stroke and shoots 3 from the tee. From the fairway, he shoots his fourth shot into the rough and loses the ball. He drops a ball at spot (X), adds a penalty stroke, and shoots stroke 6.

Unplayable Ball

If a ball lies in any position in which you believe play of the ball is impossible (such as lying against a tree, a boulder, or an out-of-bounds fence), you may declare the ball unplayable. You are the sole judge as to when your ball is unplayable. The ball may be declared unplayable at any place on the course, except in a water hazard. After declaring a ball unplayable, a player may proceed under one of the following options:

- Play the next stroke at the spot from which the original ball was played, under penalty of one stroke. (Stroke and distance penalty).
- Drop the ball within two club-lengths of the unplayable position, but not nearer the hole, under penalty of one stroke. (If the unplayable ball lies in a bunker, the ball must be dropped in the bunker.)
- Drop a ball any distance behind the unplayable position, keeping that point between the player and the hole, under penalty of one stroke. (If the unplayable ball lies in the bunker, the ball must be dropped in the bunker.)

HANDICAPS

A handicap is a number representing approximately the strokes a player shoots over par for a round. For instance, players with low handicaps, 6 and under, are excellent golfers and shoot low scores; players with high handicaps, 30 and above, shoot fairly high scores. A player with a handicap of 0 averages near par and is called a scratch golfer.

To establish a handicap a given number of rounds are played, usually 20. Score cards are turned in to the golf club or association and the handicap is figured from the 10 lowest scores of the 20.

Handicaps are used to equalize competitive play. In an 18-hole stroke play handicap event, a net score is computed for each player by subtracting his handicap from the actual (gross) score. The player with the low net score is the winner.

In match play the player with the higher handicap is allowed to subtract from his score on certain holes. For example, two opponents have handicaps of 7 and 4. The player with the 7 handicap subtracts one stroke from each of his scores on the three holes with a handicap rating of 1, 2, and 3. On the score card (Ch. 1, fig. 1.2), the three holes rated most difficult are #6, #14, and #9 for men, and #3, #17, and #5 for women. The player with the handicap of 4 gives the 7 handicapper one stroke on each of these holes, if the full handicap difference is allowed.

Honest and up-to-date handicaps make competition between players of unequal ability possible and enjoyable.

SELECTION OF EQUIPMENT AND ACCESSORIES

The first and most important consideration in selecting equipment is to have clubs that fit you. Without them, you cannot play your best golf. Your strength, bodybuild, and swing are some factors to consider. Before buying any clubs, take time to talk with one or more golf professionals or trained salespersons. They will give you extensive information. After talking with you and checking your swing, they can make a judgment as to what clubs suit you best; these services are free. You can be an intelligent buyer of clubs that fit you well.

For those people just beginning to play golf, a starter set consisting of seven clubs is adequate: woods, 1 and 3 (or 4); irons, 3, 5, 7, and 9; and putter. Playing with fewer clubs makes the game less complicated and will not deter progress in developing skill. Both new and used sets are available at reasonable prices.

The many manufacturers of golf clubs offer players a great variety of matched sets of woods and irons. Also, at most golf shops good used matched sets are for sale. Players wishing to buy matched sets have a wide choice, in different styles and in costs. Generally, the more expensive clubs will have more "feel." Higher quality material is used in the construction, and the time is taken to match shafts and clubheads to ensure balance and weights.

Because of the differences in height, strength, and hand size between men and women, men's clubs are longer, have stronger and stiffer shafts, have larger grips, and are heavier. Average golfers will find the medium shaft best suit their needs. The person with above average power and strength might find a shaft stiffer than medium better, while a person with average or less strength and power may be helped by a more flexible shaft.

Two weight measurements are considered in fitting clubs—total weight and swingweight. Simply stated, swingweight is a measurement of the clubhead weight in proportion to the shaft and grip weight. This proportional relationship between the weight of the clubhead and the combined weight of the shaft and grip is an important factor in the "feel" of the club and of the flexing of the shaft during the swing.

Much experimentation, testing, and research are being done in designing and manufacturing clubs. New concepts in club construction such as shaft length, shaft weight and flexibility, clubhead design, and swingweight continue to be introduced into the golf club market. Your best source for information on current and new developments in golf club technology is your golf professional.

Choose a putter that you like. Most golf shops will allow you to try out a putter, that is, to use and test it on their practice putting green or on an indoor putting mat. A selection can be made from a wide variety of new and used putters.

Golf balls vary in compression. For the expert, long-hitting player a high compression ball (rated near 100) is preferred. Average golfers will find lower compression balls more suitable to their games. Balls with cut-resistant covers are favored by many players.

If you plan on walking the course and carrying your clubs, choose a light-weight bag with good balance. A variety of golf bags are available—select one that best suits your needs. Hand carts are popular accessory items. Hand carts and motorized carts can be rented at most courses.

The preferred shoes for playing are golf shoes with spikes or with some kind of "traction" soles. They will help you maintain your balance in swinging and also will make walking on the course easy. Low-heeled shoes must always be worn on the course. Many players wear either a glove on the left hand or gloves on both hands. Gloves may be an aid in holding the club or in preventing blisters or callouses from forming on the hands. Wearing a hat or visor provides protection from the sun.

Comfortable and appropriate sports clothes should be worn for golf. Complete lines of attractive golf clothes for men and women are sold in many stores and in golf shops at courses.

REVIEW QUESTIONS

1. What rule options does a player have in the following situations: a ball is lost in a water hazard; a ball is lost in a lateral water hazard; a ball is lying in a tree trunk and impossible to play; a ball is lost in the rough.

2. How should you mark and lift your ball if it lies in another player's line of putt? What is the proper way to attend the flagstick?

3. Some players mistakenly state that the penalty for hitting a ball out of bounds is two strokes. What is the difference between a two stroke penalty and the stroke and distance penalty? What are some examples of rule violations that incur a two stroke penalty?

4. State at least six points of etiquette that players should observe to help keep the course in good condition. State at least five points of etiquette to be observed on the putting green.

an afterword
you and the game of golf

Nearly 100 years ago a British writer and golfer said that he would like to see an Act of Parliament that would make it compulsory for every player to go through a thorough examination on the golf rules. We might wonder what this gentleman would say about today's golfers!

Fortunately, most players do show respect: respect for the game, respect for other players, and respect for the course. But unfortunately, some players are disrespectful. They fail to observe the golf rules and play only a version of the game. They neglect to follow the rules of etiquette; they detract from the pleasures and amenities of the fellowship of golf. Because of their slow play, they prevent more people from participating in the game. They leave the course in poor condition. They discard litter. They fail to follow simple practices that will help keep the course in good condition.

Even though we would like to do it, we cannot enact a law requiring every player to be respectful. We can, however,—each of us—make a contribution to golf by upholding and preserving the rules and traditions of this venerable game. It is hoped that you who have read this book will be proud to number yourself as one of that majority—a golfer with class and consideration.

A GOLFER'S CODE

- Accept and meet the challenges of the game.
- Play by the rules. The rules are self-enforced.
- Be aware of sharing the course with other players. Play without delay, keeping your place on the course and not holding up the play of golfers following.
- Observe the safety precautions and the rules of etiquette to the finest degree.
- Appreciate the course and do your part in helping maintain its beauty.

May your actions show your appreciation of the game and contribute to the recreation and pleasure of all golfers. May your participation in this fine pastime be one of success and pleasure.

glossary of terms

Ace. A hole in one.

Addressing the ball. Taking the stance and grounding the club, except that in a hazard a player has addressed the ball when he has taken his stance.

All square. A term used in match play to indicate that the match is tied.

Approach shot. A stroke played to the putting green.

Apron. The area surrounding the putting green.

Away. The ball lying farthest from the hole.

Back 9. The last 9 holes of an 18-hole course, also *In 9*.

Backspin. A reverse spin of the ball in the vertical plane.

Banana ball. A slice.

Barranca. A deep ravine. (Spanish)

Bite. The backspin on the ball causing it to stop upon landing on the ground.

Birdie. A score of one under par for a hole.

Bogey. Commonly used to describe a score of one over par for a hole.

Brassie. The 2-wood.

Break of green. The slant or slope of the putting green.

Bunker. Usually a depressed area covered with sand, commonly called a sand trap.

Caddie. A person who carries the clubs and otherwise assists a player as the rules provide.

Casual water. A temporary accumulation of water, except in a water hazard.

Chip shot. A short, low shot played to the putting green. Also called a run-up shot.

Cup. Term commonly used for the hole on the putting green.

Curtis Cup Matches. International team matches between women amateurs of Great Britain and United States.

Divot. A piece of turf cut or displaced in making a stroke. Should be replaced and pressed down.

Dogleg. A hole in which the fairway curves to the right or left.

Dormie. A term used in match play. A player is dormie when he is as many holes up as there are holes remaining to be played.

Double bogey.   A term in common use to describe a score of two over par for a hole.

Double eagle.   A score of three under par for a hole.

Draw.   A shot that curves slightly in flight from right to left.

Driver.   The 1-wood.

Dub.   An unskilled golfer; or, to hit a poor shot.

Duffer.   A player with poor skill.

Eagle.   A score of two under par for a hole.

Explosion shot.   A shot played from a sand trap. An attempt is made to swing the club through the sand well back of the ball.

Fade.   A shot that curves slightly in flight from left to right.

Fairway.   The mowed grassy area between the tee and putting green.

Fat shot.   A shot in which the ground is struck before contacting the ball, usually resulting in a poor shot.

Fellow-competitor.   In stroke play, any person with whom the competitor plays.

Flagstick.   The marker which indicates location of the hole.

Flat swing.   A swing in which the club is swung in a low arc. At the top of the backswing the club shaft is lower than the orthodox swing.

Flub.   A poorly hit shot; or, to hit a poor shot.

Fore!.   A warning cry to anyone who might be endangered by a golf shot.

Foursome.   Four players playing together who may or may not be engaged in a match.

Frog hair.   The grass surrounding the putting green.

Front 9.   The first 9 holes of an 18-hole course, also *Out 9.*

Gross score.   The actual total score for a round.

Ground under repair.   Staked or lined area on which work is being done. A ball coming to rest in an area may be lifted and dropped in accordance with rules.

Grounding the club.   Placing the sole of the club on the ground in preparation for making the stroke.

Halved or halving a hole.   In match play, to tie a hole.

Handicap.   The approximate number of strokes one shoots over par, or the allowance of strokes to equalize players of different ability.

Hazard.   By USGA definitions, bunkers and water hazards.

High handicapper.   A player who shoots many strokes over par, an unskilled player.

Hole.   (1) the receptacle on the putting green 4¼ inches in diameter and at least 4 inches deep; (2) one unit or division of the course.

Hole high.   The ball is in a position as far as the hole but off to either side of it.

Hole out.   To complete the play of a hole.

Hook.   A ball that curves in flight to the left due to a horizontal, counterclockwise spin on the ball.

Honor.   The privilege of hitting first from the tee.

In 9.   The second 9 holes of an 18-hole course, also *Back 9.*

LPGA.   Ladies Professional Golf Association.

Lateral Water Hazard.   A water hazard running approximately parallel to the line of play.

Lie.   The position of the ball on the ground.

Loft of club.   The angle of pitch of the clubface.

Loose impediments.   Objects such as dead grass and fallen leaves, pebbles, worms, fallen twigs.

Low handicapper.   A skilled golfer who shoots near par.

Mashie.   The 5-iron.

Match play.   Competition based on scores for each hole rather than total score.

Medal play.   More commonly called stroke play. Competition by total score.

Medalist.   The player with the lowest score for a qualifying round of a match play tournament.

Metal woods.   "Wood" clubs with clubheads constructed of metal, such as stainless steel or aluminum.

Mid-iron.   The 2-iron.

Mixed foursome.   A group of four players made up of two women and two men.

Mulligan.   An illegal practice of taking a second drive from the first tee without penalty if the first shot is a poor one.

Nassau scoring system.   A system of scoring allowing one point to the winner of each 9 holes and one point for the match.

Net score.   A score resulting from subtraction of the handicap from the gross score.

Niblick.   The 9-iron.

Obstruction.   An artificial object on the course which may be movable or fixed.

On the beach.   In the sand trap.

Open tournament.   A competitive event in which both amateurs and professionals play, such as The United States Open Championship and The Open Championship of the British Isles.

Opponent.   The player opposing you in a match.

Out 9.   The first 9 holes of an 18-hole course, also *Front 9.*

Out of Bounds.   Ground on which play is prohibited, usually marked by out of bounds stakes or fences.

PGA.   Professional Golfer's Association

Par.   An arbitrary standard of scoring excellence based on the length of a hole allowing two putts on the putting green.

Pin high.   Same as hole high.

Pitch shot.   A shot that travels in a high trajectory played to the putting green.

Press.   Attempting to hit the ball beyond one's normal power.

Pronation.   An anatomical term to describe the turning of the hand and forearm inward. Supination is the opposite action in which the hand and forearm are turned out so the palm is facing up.

Provisional ball.   A second ball played in case the first ball is or is thought to be lost outside a water hazard or out of bounds.

Pull.   A shot that travels to the left of the intended line.

Push.   A shot that travels in a straight line, but to the right of the intended target.

Quail high.   Low flying shot.

Rainmaker.   Shot with a very high trajectory.

Rough.   The areas bordering the fairway in which the grass, weeds, etc., are allowed to grow freely.

Royal and Ancient Golf Club of St. Andrews, Scotland. (The R and A) The governing body of golf in Great Britain.

Rub of the green. An unpredictable happening to the ball when the ball in motion or at rest is stopped or deflected by an outside agency.

Ryder Cup Matches. Competition between two men's professional teams: Great Britain and Europe team matched against the United States team.

Sand trap. The term commonly applied to a bunker.

Scotch foursome. A match in which partners compete. Each partnership of two plays alternate strokes using one ball.

Scratch player. A player who has a handicap of 0, shooting consistently near par.

Slice. A shot that curves in flight to the right, caused by the ball spinning in a horizontal, clockwise manner.

Spoon. The 3-wood.

Stance. The position of the feet in addressing the ball.

Stroke play. Competition by total strokes.

Stymie. To have another player's golf ball or some object blocking one's line of play—to be stymied. Also an obsolete rule of golf.

Summer rules. Term sometimes used to describe play disallowing "winter rules."

Tee. The starting place for a hole; or, the peg on which the ball is placed for driving.

Tee markers. The markers placed on the tee to indicate the forward limits of the teeing area.

Texas wedge. A name applied to the putter when it is used to play any shot from off the putting green.

Through the green. This is the whole of the course, except the teeing ground and putting green of the hole being played and all hazards.

Underclubbing. Using a club that will not give enough distance for the desired shot. For instance, using a 7-iron when a 6-iron or 5-iron should be used—a more common error than over-clubbing.

Up and down. Holing out in 2 strokes from off the green.

Upright swing. A swing in which the club is swung high into the air on the backswing and follow-through. The opposite of a flat swing.

USGA. The United States Golf Association—governing body of golf in the U.S.A.

Walker Cup Matches. Matches between men amateurs of Great Britain and the United States.

Whiff. To swing at the ball and miss it completely—to fan.

Winter rules. Special local rules which permit the ball to be moved to a better lie on the fairway; also called "preferred lies."

questions and answers

TRUE-FALSE

1. When you play golf, be aware of keeping your place on the course. If your group is playing slowly and not keeping its place, either urge your foursome to catch up and maintain its position, or invite the following group to play through.

2. To hit a good iron shot you should take a divot. Therefore, when you take a practice swing, be sure and take a divot.

3. It is all right to leave your golf bag (or golf bag and cart) at the front of the green, if you hurry to move the golf bag when you have completed play of the hole.

4. If you hit a ball that is travelling toward someone and may endanger that person, immediately call "FORE!" loudly. At your earliest convenience, express your apology to that person.

5. If you tee off first and your drive goes far off line into the wrong fairway or rough, to speed up play, pick up your clubs and hurry to your shot while your playing companions are teeing off.

6. It is good practice to mark and lift your ball before each putt you play.

7. Players should record their scores on the score card before they leave the putting green.

8. If a group fails to keep its place on the course, losing more than one clear hole on the group in front, the slow group should allow the following group to play through.

9. When you attend the flagstick, stand to the left side of the hole and hold the stick and pennant with your right hand.

10. If a player in your group is having trouble with his game, watch his swing and volunteer some tips to improve his game.

11. When your group has finished playing a hole, replace the flagstick and leave the green immediately. Do not stand on the green to review play of the hole or to mark scores on the score card.

12. When you attend the flagstick, hold both the stick and the banner, with the stick remaining in the cup (until removal is necessary). Stand to one side of the hole and be sure that your shadow is not cast across the player's line of putt.

13. All divots should be replaced and pressed firmly in place.

14. Watch the shot results of players in your group, so that if necessary, you can help in the search for a ball.

15. If you hit your ball into the wrong fairway, you do not have the right-of-way. Before entering that fairway, be certain it is safe to do so, and be sure you do not interfere with golfers playing down that fairway.

16. After playing a shot from a bunker, a player should rake the sand and leave the surface as good or better than he found it.

17. Pit marks and damage made by balls landing on the green should be repaired. This includes any scarred spot, not just the one made by the player.

18. In stroke play, contestants with whom one plays are called fellow-competitors. In match play competition, the contestant one plays against is called the opponent.

19. "Through the green" is a term referring to all of the course, except the tee and the putting green being played, and all hazards.

20. If a ball lies so any part of it is touching the putting green, the ball is deemed to be on the putting green.

21. The ball must lie wholly on the putting green to be considered on the green.

22. A player has addressed the ball when the stance has been taken and the club grounded. Except, in a hazard the player has addressed the ball when the stance has been taken.

23. The penalty for waiving a rule is one stroke in stroke and match play.

24. The penalty for waiving a rule in any play is disqualification.

25. Golf rules are too complex to master, so in a friendly game where players are out to have fun, the rules may be changed to suit the players.

26. The penalty for waiving a rule is 2 strokes in stroke play and loss of hole in match play.

27. The general penalty for breach of a rule in match play is loss of hole.

28. The general penalty for breach of a rule in match play is one stroke.

29. The greatest margin by which a player can win an 18-hole match is 10–8.

30. Match play. Player A, before playing a shot from a bunker, lifts a fallen leaf from the sand. Player A immediately loses the hole to his opponent.

31. Player A is dormie 2. A loses the next 2 holes, so is now 4 holes down.

32. Player A is dormie 6. A wins the next hole, thus winning the match 7–5.

33. To win an 18-hole match, a player must have a lower total score than the opponent.

34. The general penalty for breach of a rule in stroke play is one stroke.

35. The general penalty for breach of a rule in stroke play is two strokes.

36. Stroke play. Player A's ball lies 4 inches from the hole. Player B's ball lies 3 feet from the cup. Player B may concede the putt to Player A in tournament play.

37. Stroke play. A player stamps down the surface of the putting green in his line of putt. The penalty is 2 strokes.

38. Stroke play. On the fairway, a player pulls out a dandelion growing back of the ball. The penalty is one stroke.

39. In a friendly game, borrowing a club from another player is common and accepted practice.

40. The shaft of the putter may be attached to any point in the clubhead.

41. There is no limit as to how many clubs a player may carry in a round of golf.

42. If a player unduly delays play after completing the fifth hole and before starting play on the sixth tee, the penalty is one stroke in both stroke and match play. The penalty is assessed on the sixth hole.

43. If a player unduly delays play at the end of the fifth hole and before teeing off on the sixth hole, the penalty is 2 strokes in stroke play and loss of hole in match play. The penalty is assessed on the sixth hole.

44. A practice swing may be taken at any place on the course, provided the player does not violate any rules applying to the area.

45. A practive swing may NOT be taken within the boundaries of a hazard.

46. Match play. During the play of a hole, Player A plays a practice shot to the putting green. A loses the hole immediately.

47. Match play. Player A asks her opponent, B, what club she used for a particular shot. Player B declares that she has won the hole because of the rule violation by A. B is correct.

48. Stroke play. You are allowed to ask your caddie or your fellow-competitor for advice.

49. If you are playing a stroke to the putting green and cannot see the flagstick, you are permitted to ask a member of your foursome to stand in and remain in the correct line to the hole, until you play your shot.

50. Stroke play. You ask your fellow-competitor for advice. You are penalized 2 strokes.

51. A foursome played from the first tee in this order: A, B, C, and D. The scores for the hole were: A-6, B-4, C-5, and D-4. On the second hole the players should tee off in this order: D, B, C, and A.

52. Stroke play. A player fails to play according to honor. The penalty is 2 strokes and the ball remains in play.

53. Stroke play. A player fails to play according to honor. There is no penalty. The ball remains in play.

54. Match play. You fail to play according to honor. There is no penalty. Your opponent may either require you to play another ball, or allow you to continue play with the original ball.

55. Match play. You fail to play according to honor. The penalty is loss of hole.

56. Player A's ball is on the putting green 60 feet from the hole. B's ball is lying off the green 50 feet from the hole. The rules state that Player A should play first because his ball is farther from the hole.

57. Stroke play. A competitor plays his approach shot to the putting green out of turn. The penalty is 2 strokes.

58. Match play. Your ball is farther from the hole than your opponent's ball; however, your opponent plays before you do. You win the hole.

59. The teeing ground, the starting place for a hole, is a rectangular area extending 2 club lengths back of the tee markers. The front and sides are defined by the outside limits of the markers.

60. The teeing ground is bounded in front by tee markers and extends one club length back of the markers.

61. Match play. The penalty for teeing and playing a ball from outside the limits of the teeing area is loss of hole.

62. Match play. There is no penalty for teeing and playing a ball from outside the teeing area, but your opponent may require you to replay the shot from within the teeing area.

63. Stroke play. Any first stroke played from outside the teeing ground does not count. The player is penalized 2 strokes, and then must play a ball from within the teeing area.

64. Stroke play. Player A plays her first stroke from outside the teeing area. She must count that stroke and shoot stroke 2 from within the teeing area.

65. If a player's ball comes to rest on sandy soil on the fairway, he is allowed to brush aside the sand back of the ball.

66. Stroke play. A player accidentally grounds her club in the sand trap. The penalty is one stroke.

67. Stroke play. A player purposely grounds his club in a sand trap. The penalty is 2 strokes.

68. Match play. Before playing a shot from under a tree, a player breaks a small limb from the tree. The penalty is loss of hole.

69. Stroke play. A player plays a wrong ball from a bunker and then discovers her mistake. The player then plays the correct ball. The stroke played with the wrong ball does not count. There is no penalty for having played the wrong ball.

70. Match play. Your opponent plays the wrong ball from the fairway. You win the hole.

71. You play the wrong ball from the rough in stroke play and then discover your mistake. You add 2 penalty strokes to your score for the hole; you do not count the one stroke played with the wrong ball; then you play the correct ball.

72. A ball lying on the putting green may always be lifted and cleaned without penalty.

73. Any sand, loose soil, or loose impediments may be removed from the putting green. If a player moves the ball in removing such impediments, the ball must be replaced. There is no penalty.

74. You may take any type stance to putt a ball lying on or off the putting green.

75. Match play. You may concede putts to your opponent.

76. Stroke play. A player holes a short putt with the handle of the putter. The penalty is one stroke.

77. Marks or damage caused by the impact of the ball on the putting green may be repaired, but only when the player's ball lies on the green.

78. If a player's ball overhangs the edge of the cup, the player after walking to the hole without delay, may wait an additional 10 seconds for the ball to drop into the hole. If the ball does not fall into the cup in that time, the ball is deemed to be at rest.

79. If a player's ball overhangs the edge of the cup, the player after walking to the hole without delay, may wait 30 seconds for the ball to drop into the hole. If the ball does not fall into the cup in that time, it is deemed to be at rest.

80. Stroke play. Your ball is 3 feet off the putting green. You use your putter to stroke the ball and the ball strikes the unattended flagstick. There is no penalty.

81. If you stroke your ball from the putting green and the ball strikes the unattended flagstick, the penalty is loss of hole in match play and 2 strokes in stroke play.

82. If you are playing a shot to the putting green and you cannot see the flagstick, you may have the stick held up to indicate the position of the hole.

83. When you are playing a putt from the putting green, you should either request that the flagstick be attended or removed from the hole.

84. Match play. Your opponent is attending the flagstick. You putt your ball from the green and the ball strikes the stick. Your opponent immediately loses the hole.

85. Match play. Both balls on putting green. Player A putts his ball and it strikes Player B's ball. Player A loses the hole.

86. Stroke play. Balls on putting green. Your fellow-competitor putts and his ball strikes and moves your ball. You must replace your ball to its original position. Your fellow-competitor must add 2 strokes to his score for the hole.

87. Match play. Both balls on putting green. Player A putts and his ball strikes and knocks B's ball into the hole. Player A loses the hole.

88. Stroke play. Par-3 hole. Both players have reached the green in one shot. Player A putts and his ball strikes and knocks B's ball into the hole. Player B must lift his ball from the hole and place it in its original position. Player A is penalized 2 strokes.

89. Match play. Both balls on putting green. Your opponent's ball strikes your ball and moves it closer to the hole. You must replace your ball. Your opponent is not penalized.

90. If in addressing the ball (not in play) on the tee, a player accidentally knocks the ball off the tee, the ball may be re-teed without penalty.

91. If in addressing any golf shot, the player accidentally moves the ball, the penalty is one stroke.

92. If in addressing the ball in play, you accidentally move the ball, the penalty is one stroke and you must play the ball as it lies.

93. Stroke play. Your fellow-competitor is helping you search for your ball, and he accidentally moves your ball. There is no penalty. You must replace your ball to the spot from which it was moved.

94. Stroke play. Balls on putting green. If your fellow-competitor considers that your ball may interfere with his stroke, he may request that you mark your ball. At your option, you may either mark or play the ball.

95. The following are some typical loose impediments: stones (not solidly imbedded); fallen twigs, leaves, and branches; worms and insects.

96. Loose impediments may be removed from any place on the course.

97. If you move a loose impediment lying within one club-length of your ball on the fairway and the ball moves, the penalty is 2 strokes and the ball must be played as it lies.

98. Through the green, if you move a loose impediment lying within one club-length of your ball and the ball moves before you address it, the penalty is one stroke and you must replace the ball.

99. You may NOT remove loose impediments from a hazard when your ball lies in the hazard.

100. Sand and loose soil are loose impediments on the putting green only.

101. If through the green, immovable obstructions such as ball washers, sprinkler heads, benches, protective screens, or paved cart paths interfere with your stance or the area of your intended swing, you may, without penalty, lift and drop your ball within one club-length of the nearest point of relief from the condition, but not nearer the hole.

102. Movable obstructions such as rakes, trash containers, and hoses may always be moved if they interfere with play.

103. You may NOT lift and drop the ball away from out-of-bounds fences or stakes that interfere with play without penalty.

104. Through the green, your ball lies in casual water. Without penalty, you may lift and drop the ball within one club-length of the nearest point of relief, but not nearer the hole.

105. Your ball comes to rest in a sand trap completely filled with casual water. You are permitted to drop the ball outside the hazard, not nearer the hole, without penalty.

106. If casual water on the putting green intervenes between your ball (lying on the green) and the hole, you may lift and place your ball at the nearest position giving you relief, but not nearer the hole. There is no penalty.

107. Your ball lies 10 feet off the putting green. There is casual water on the green between your ball and the hole. You may lift and drop the ball, not nearer the hole, avoiding the interference of the casual water.

108. Your ball lies on the wrong putting green. You must lift and drop the ball off the green within one club-length of the nearest point of relief, not nearer the hole, without penalty.

109. Your ball lies on the wrong putting green. You may lift and drop the ball off the green 2 club-lengths from the nearest point of relief, not nearer the hole, without penalty.

110. If you lift a ball from a water hazard, under penalty of one stroke, you may drop the ball any distance back of the hazard, keeping the spot where the ball last crossed the margin of the hazard between yourself and the hole.

111. If you hit your tee shot into a creek running across the fairway, you may play another ball from the tee under penalty of one stroke.

112. You hit your ball into a lateral water hazard. It is impossible to play the ball. Your only option is to drop a ball within 2 club-lengths of the margin of either side of the hazard, opposite the point where the ball last crossed the hazard and not nearer the hole. The penalty is one stroke.

113. The penalty for hitting a ball out of bounds or for losing a ball outside a water hazard is 2 strokes.

114. A player hits his third shot from a position 200 yards from the green. The ball travels into the rough and is not found. The player may drop a ball on the fairway at the spot where the ball entered the rough and add one penalty stroke to his score for the hole.

115. You hit your drive from the tee over an out-of-bounds fence. You must drive again from the tee, and you are shooting stroke 2.

116. After hitting your ball out of bounds from the tee, you tee another ball and you are shooting stroke 3.

117. The penalty for hitting a ball out of bounds or for losing a ball outside a water hazard is one stroke and distance.

118. You may stand out of bounds to hit a ball lying in bounds.

119. You are allowed 3 minutes to search for a ball.

120. You are allowed 5 minutes to search for a ball.

121. A provisional ball may be played if a ball may be lost outside a water hazard or may be out of bounds.

122. A provisional ball may be played if a player believes the ball may be lost outside a water hazard, out of bounds, or unplayable.

123. A player hits her second shot into a bunker and declares the ball unplayable. She selects the option of dropping the ball behind the unplayable position. She is allowed to drop the ball out of the hazard, (any distance back of the unplayable spot) provided she keeps the unplayable spot between herself and the hole. After the drop she is shooting 4.

124. A player finds his tee shot in the trunk of a tree. He declares the ball unplayable. He may proceed under three options: (a) go back to the tee and shoot stroke 3; (b) drop a ball within 2 club-lengths of the unplayable position (not nearer the hole) and shoot stroke 3; (c) drop a ball any distance back of the unplayable position (keeping the spot where the ball originally lay between himself and the hole) and shoot stroke 3.

125. The player is the sole judge as to when his ball is unplayable. The ball may be declared unplayable at any place on the course, except in a water hazard.

COMPLETION

126. On a par-3 hole with a lake intervening between the tee and the green, a player hits 3 shots from the tee into the middle of the lake. He tees up a fourth ball and hits it on to the green and it rolls into the hole. His score for the hole is _____ .

127. A player drives out of bounds from the tee. He tees another ball and in addressing the ball accidentally knocks the ball off the tee. He re-tees the ball. He is shooting stroke _____ .

128–129. A player drives out of bounds from the tee. She tees another ball and hits it into the rough 150 yards from the hole. After a search she declares the ball is lost. She must play another ball from _____ , and is shooting stroke _____ .

130. Stroke play. A player's ball lies 3 in the bunker adjacent to the green. Before striking the fourth shot, the player accidentally touches the sand with the clubhead in addressing the ball. She hits the ball and it lands on the green and rolls into the cup. Her score for the hole is _____ .

131. A player hits his tee shot out of bounds. He tees another ball, and then stamps down the grass back of the ball. He hits the ball into a creek running across the fairway 10 yards from the tee. He tees up another ball and drives 180 yards down the fairway. His score up to this point is _____ .

132–133. A player hits her drive into a fairway hillside. She addresses the ball, and it rolls 5 feet down the hillside. She must (a) play the ball as it lies or (b) replace the ball [choose (a) or (b)] _____ , and is shooting stroke number _____ .

134–135. A player's ball lies 3 on the putting green. In brushing away sand from near the ball with the putterhead, she accidentally moves the ball. She must either (a) replace the ball, or (b) leave the ball where it comes to rest [choose (a) or (b)] _____ . She holes her putt and scores _____ on the hole.

136. A player's ball lies 4 in the rough. Before addressing the ball, she removes a dead twig lying within one club-length of the ball. As this player starts her backswing to hit the ball, the ball moves. The player continues her swing and strikes the ball onto the green. She takes 2 putts and scores _____ on the hole.

137. A player hits her second shot, and the ball comes to rest in casual water in a bunker. She drops the ball outside the bunker (not nearer the hole and keeping the spot where the ball lay between herself and the hole). She hits the ball onto the green and takes one putt. Her score for the hole is _____ .

138–139. Player A's ball lies 3 on the putting green, 60 feet from the hole. His fellow-competitor's ball lies 3 feet from the hole. Player A putts and his ball strikes and moves B's ball to a position 4 feet from the cup. Player B must either (a) leave his ball 4 feet from the hole, or (b) replace the ball to the position 3 feet from the cup [choose (a) or (b)] _____ . Player A strokes his next putt into the hole and scores _____ for the hole.

140. A player's ball lies 3 feet off the green in 2 strokes. There is a spot of mud adhering to the top of the ball. The player, without moving the ball, wipes off the mud. He then chips the ball onto the green and takes one putt. His score for the hole is _____ .

141. A score of two under par for a hole is a/an _____ .

142. A score of one over par for a hole is commonly called a/an _____ .

143. A score of one under par for a hole is a/an _____ .

144. A golf shot that curves in flight to the left (for right-handers) is called a/an _____ .

145. The last nine holes of an 18-hole course is called _____ .

146. The first nine holes of an 18-hole course is called _____ .

147. In order for a ball to curve in flight (disregarding any wind factor) the ball must be hit so it spins. In a slice the ball spins _____ .

148. A hole in which the fairway curves to the right or left is called a/an _____ .

149. Par for a hole 375 yards in length is _____ .

150. Par for a hole 200 yards in length is _____ .

151. Par for a hole 525 yards in length is _____ .

152. The general penalty for breach of a rule in stroke play is _____ .

153. The penalty for losing a ball outside of a water hazard is _____ .

154. To drop a ball correctly, the player must _____ .

155. The total number of clubs a player may carry in a round is _____ .

156. The length of time a player is allowed to search for a ball is _____ .

157. In a correct and effective shot the path of the clubhead through the contact area should be _____ .

158. The most widely used golf grip for all strokes (putting excepted) is the _____ .

159. Your ball is lying in a deep sand trap adjacent to the putting green. There is an overhanging lip on the bunker. Your best choice of club for this shot is _____ .

160. A piece of turf cut or displaced in making a stroke (which should be replaced) is a/an _____ .

161. A stance in which the right foot is placed nearer the intended line of flight than the left foot is called a/an _____ .

162. A stance in which the left foot is placed nearer the intended line of flight than the right foot is called a/an _____ .

163. A second ball played in case the first ball is or is thought to be out of bounds or lost outside a water hazard is a/an _____ .

164. If you can hit a ball 150 yards with a #5-iron, approximately what distance can you expect to hit a ball with a #3-iron? _____ .

165. If you can hit a ball 110 yards with a #7-iron, approximately what distance can you expect to hit a ball with a #5-iron? _____ .

166. Your ball is lying in a sand trap adjacent to the green. The ball is sitting well up on the firm sand, and there is no overhanging turf on the shallow trap. The grass on the apron is cut short. What is your best choice of club for this shot? _____ .

167. Your ball is in a sidehill-uphill lie. You must stand so one foot is higher than the other. Will you play the ball from a spot more opposite the lower foot or higher foot? _____ .

168. In the overlapping, interlocking, or 10-finger grips the V's formed by the thumbs and index fingers should point approximately toward the _____ .

169. The penalty for lifting a ball from a water hazard or losing a ball in a water hazard is _____ .

170. When you finish play of a hole, why should you leave the green immediately and proceed to the next tee? _____ .

171. To hit a straight golf shot to a target, what must the relationship be between the clubface and club path at impact? _____ .

172. You are topping shots with the long irons and fairways woods, but not with the medium irons. What steps would you take to correct the error? _____ .

173. Joe is playing his first round of golf. His golf ball comes to rest in a deep bunker adjacent to the green. On his fourth attempt to hit the ball from the trap, he hits the ball well past the green into another deep bunker. The foursome following is waiting out on the fairway. What would you do if you were Joe? _____ .

174. You wish to hit a shot so it will curve in flight to the left. By changing your hold on the club you may affect the ball flight. How will you change your hand position for this shot? _____ .

175. You are planning to purchase a minimum set of seven clubs. What is the best selection of clubs you can make for a 7-club set? _____ .

QUESTION ANSWER KEY

True and False

1. T	26. F	51. F	76. F	101. T
2. F	27. T	52. F	77. F	102. T
3. F	28. F	53. T	78. T	103. T
4. T	29. T	54. T	79. F	104. T
5. F	30. T	55. F	80. T	105. F
6. F	31. F	56. T	81. T	106. T
7. F	32. T	57. F	82. T	107. F
8. T	33. F	58. F	83. T	108. T
9. F	34. F	59. T	84. F	109. F
10. F	35. T	60. F	85. F	110. T
11. T	36. F	61. F	86. T	111. T
12. T	37. T	62. T	87. F	112. F
13. T	38. F	63. T	88. T	113. F
14. T	39. F	64. F	89. T	114. F
15. T	40. T	65. F	90. T	115. F
16. T	41. F	66. F	91. F	116. T
17. T	42. F	67. T	92. T	117. T
18. T	43. T	68. T	93. T	118. T
19. T	44. T	69. T	94. T	119. F
20. T	45. F	70. T	95. T	120. T
21. F	46. T	71. T	96. F	121. T
22. T	47. T	72. T	97. F	122. F
23. F	48. F	73. T	98. T	123. F
24. T	49. F	74. F	99. T	124. T
25. F	50. T	75. T	100. T	125. T

Completion

126. 7
127. 3
128. the tee
129. 5
130. 6
131. 5
132. (a) play the ball as it lies
133. 3
134. (a) replace the ball
135. 4
136. 8
137. 5
138. (b) replace the ball
139. 6
140. 5
141. eagle
142. bogey

143. birdie
144. hook or draw
145. in or back 9
146. out or front 9
147. clockwise
148. dogleg
149. 4
150. 3
151. 5
152. 2 strokes
153. one stroke and distance
154. stand erect, hold the ball at arm's length and shoulder height, and drop it
155. 14
156. 5 minutes
157. from inside the intended line of flight, on the intended line, and inside the line
158. overlapping grip
159. wedge or high lofted iron
160. divot
161. open stance
162. closed stance
163. provisional ball
164. 170 yards
165. 130 yards
166. putter, or iron to chip the ball from the trap
167. higher foot
168. right shoulder
169. one stroke
170. to avoid delaying play and for your safety
171. clubhead must be travelling on intended line of ball flight with the clubface perpendicular to the line.
172. swing clubhead low to ground, try to hit *low shots,* alternate between hitting shots with the medium irons and longer clubs.
173. pick up the ball and discontinue play of this hole. Resume play at next tee. Better days are coming.
174. right palm facing more skyward, and left palm facing more towards the ground
175. #1 and 3 (or 4) woods, #3, 5, 7, and 9 irons, and putter

index